Undecided
Neti-Neti

KARL RENZ

Undecided
Neti-Neti

Karl Renz

Edited By
Manjit Achhra

A Division of Maoli Media Private Limited

Are you the Self? Negative.
Are you not the Self? Negative.
Are you God? Negative.
Are you not God? Negative.
That's called Undecided.

Karl Renz

Undecided: Neti-Neti

Copyright © 2015 Karl Renz

First Edition: November 2015

PUBLISHED BY
ZEN PUBLICATIONS
A Division of Maoli Media Private Limited

60, Juhu Supreme Shopping Centre,
Gulmohar Cross Road No. 9, JVPD Scheme,
Juhu, Mumbai 400 049. India.

Tel: +91 9022208074
eMail: info@zenpublications.com
Website: www.zenpublications.com

Book Design: Red Sky Designs, Mumbai
Cover Image: Detail of a painting by Karl Renz

ISBN   978-93-84363-98-7

All rights reserved. No part of this book may be reproduced or transmitted in any form or by any means, electronic or mechanical, including photocopying, recording, or by any information storage and retrieval system without written permission from the author or his agents, except for the inclusion of brief quotations in a review.

Contents

Your Existence Never Demands Any Definition Or Understanding	11
Many Answers, Many Questions And Nothing Happens	45
As Long As A Teacher Has Something To Teach, He Has Something To Learn.	75
The Absolute Gift Is That What-You-Are Needs Nothing – Not Even 'Nothing'!	107
Hope Is For The Spiritual Kindergarten, To Make The Kids Quiet	136
Bhakta And Jñani Are Two Different Names Of Absolute Non-Ownership	160
On That You Can Rely, That Everything Is A Lie	187
Meditation Of *Neti-Neti* Means Being The Undecided	207

Other Books by Karl Renz

- A Little Bit Of Nothingness
  81 Observations On The Unnamable

- The Song of Irrelevance
  Meditation of what you are

- Heaven and Hell

- Am I - I Am

- May It Be As It Is
  The Embrace of Helplessness

- Worry and be Happy
  The Audacity of Hopelessness

- Echoes of Slience
  Avadhut Gita Revisited

- If You Wake Up, Don't Take It Personally
  Dialogues in the Presence of Arunachala

- The Myth of Enlightenment
  Seeing Through the Illusion of Separation

ACKNOWLEDGEMENT

The Publishers wish to thank
Anjali Walsh, Hemant Nadkarni and Amrita Hinduja
for their invaluable help
in making this book possible.

Your Existence Never Demands any Definition or Understanding

∽

Q: What is the difference between the 'me' that has a story and the awareness?

K: The 'me' is the definer, defining having or not-having a story. Time or no-time, it needs that one who defines time and no-time, presence or absence of a 'me'. It needs a 'me' to be not present. That there's a 'me' that's not present; it needs a 'me' who is not there, still to be there. It still needs one who experiences that there is no 'me'. So even in the absence of a 'me' there is a 'me'. When God takes himself as a relative story, he becomes a jiva. But both are relative stories. The personal or the impersonal are relative stories of a personal or an impersonal story because there is 'one' who has a story. And by accepting the personal and the impersonal story, you are That, and that is the end of story! End of the story because there is no beginning and no end, and without a beginning and end, there is no story.

Q: You mean when there are no concepts about impersonal or personal, no-story or story?

K: No-concept is still a concept.

Q: When I speak, I don't know how else to say. When there is not even an idea of no-concept or no idea of concept, no idea or no-idea about anything...

K: You can take that to infinity – no, no, no... but it still needs one who defines it.

Q: So, you are saying 'this' disappears...

K: No. There is no disappearing because there was never anything like that, that's the problem. There is an illusion of separation game of the story of the 'me'. But it was never there. There was never any reality in it. It was never alive; there was no life like that. So, it is not like it disappears, it was never there. The one who says it is an illusion, is an illusion. Life is – that's all! And there is no so-called seeing through the illusion and now I made it.

That's why this pointer of deep-deep sleep, there is a total carelessness of anything because you exist without any – no, no, no. There is no need of any definition or no-definition at all. So, the pointer is that you exist without any definer. Your existence never demands any definition or understanding or knowing or not knowing. Whatever you can give a name or frame or definition can never make you That – what never needs anything.

Q: Now I am speaking, asking and wanting to know...

K: That is self-inquiry...

Q: And you say that it just continues?

K: That is a never ending story of consciousness, which is a never ending story of meditation or self-inquiry. It will never end. The intellect will always ask itself – What is intellect? That's its nature. At the moment there is a questioner, even a potential questioner 'I', it will question that existence. Consciousness in its purest form is the root thought 'I', which questions itself.

Q: You are just stating the mechanism of consciousness and it just keeps happening...

K: It is the infinite realization of That what is Reality and realization of Reality is Reality meditating about that what is Reality, and it never started and will never end. When the Reality or Brahman or Self wakes up to awareness, already meditation happens. It's like waking up to meditation and meditation is the absolute dream of what one is. That dream never started and will never stop as the dream is not different from the dreamer. As the dreamer had no beginning, the dream has no beginning and no end. Reality is not different from realization but in realization you expect to find yourself in realization, but the Reality is already there, you cannot find it.

Q: I'm just thinking that something needs to stop...

K: Yes and no. For the relative thing what you think you are when what-you-are is what-it-is.

Q: Right now I'm questioning and I want to know...

K: Right now you committed suicide by stepping into a relative identity. That is like missing something. You are missing for the longing. Then you expect by meditation or by whatever to gain what you seemingly lost. That is dream, that's the only dream. That you think by the experience of being born, you are born. You take that as real. Then Shiva becomes a puppet because he takes the experience of being born as real. Then we sit here and ask did really something happen in that or your nature was prior to two liquids meeting and creating the experience of this body? There is nothing wrong with the experience; it's just you taking it as your home. Then you become an owner of a relative home.

Then you miss your absolute home. Then from that moment on, you try everything. Even by buying a piece of bread, you want to be happy because you are missing happiness. You are missing the happiness of the absence of the one who can be and cannot be happy. Now you became one who can be happy or unhappy. From that moment on, you miss happiness that is unconditioned in its nature; the happiness that never depends on any circumstance at all. From that moment, out of that misunderstanding, suffering starts, because missing is suffering. And no understanding in this world can satisfy you and maybe you see that in one instant: that the satisfaction which comes can never be the fulfilment you are longing for. Then maybe the 'me' drops, and suddenly there is a fulfilment without any dependency at all.

Q: What is the 'me' that drops?

K: Every night it drops.

Q: Exactly and not just at night….

K: Yeah, ninety-nine percent of the day you are in peace. There is only one percent of 'me' that is disturbed. If it is five percent, you already enter into a psychiatric hospital.

Q: So the one percent drops as well?

K: No. It pops up again with the body.

Q: So, does the 'me' drop in the dropping?

K: The 'me' cannot drop. How can that what is a phantom drop? It was never alive, how can it drop? You still make it a dependency as if something has to happen. Nothing has to happen, nothing will happen.

Q: I read in a book about the 'I-lessness. Does that mean that the 'I' drops?

K: It was never there. You existed without interruption. There was never any 'I' even as an experience. The realization was uninterrupted. There was never-never any moment without realization of Reality. Reality was uninterrupted That What-Is. There was never any 'I' or 'me' or illusion; whatever you can imagine was never there. There is nothing that has to drop and that is worse for the ego that no one needs it to go. That is the end of the ego because no one is there who needs the ego to go. It may be there or not, who cares? There is not even one who knows the ego.

Q: I cannot find That…

K: That you cannot produce because it was always there. It was never-never.

Q: I cannot find the ego...

K: If you look into it, you cannot find it for sure.

Q: I have been looking for it and cannot find it...

K: Says the ego... because it was always there, always hiding. It is always hide-and-seek. That is the game of existence, Shiva playing hide-and-seek. But there is no other Shiva he can play with, so he imagines some play mobiles. In the beginning Shiva becomes a God child and cries 'I am not there' suffering about not finding himself. Then in one instant he sees it and is happy, 'Thank God I cannot find myself; Thank God I am not a relative object in time, Thank God that there is no God'. Then the slavery ends in one instant. Then you are happy not to find yourself but you are still looking. You look for yourself and say 'Thank God I am not there. It looked so promising but I am not there'. Wonderful!

So, it is like a little switch from being a little self-pity child or having the fun of looking. But you cannot decide. You drop out of the Almighty of happiness into the self-pity of missing and you cannot avoid it. Then you need some reminders – Did something really happen? Can you really miss yourself? What kind of stupid idea can it be? Are you not here now? Can you miss yourself? Was there any moment without you? But it doesn't help and that's the beauty of it. Because even that, you will forget again.

But that there can be a forgetting, you have to exist. That there can be a remembering, you have to exist. That existence was uninterrupted what-you-are. So, nothing happened in forgetting and nothing happened in remembering. But both are like a game. But if it has to be real as it seems to be, you have to forget that you are the Almighty so that you can play as a little one who has this experience. You cannot avoid it. You cannot avoid experiencing yourself in every possible way. And one way is to experience yourself as the little one – the missing one.

You cannot avoid the missing. You cannot avoid anything. All that is realization of that what is called existence. If it could be avoided, imagine that Jesus, Buddha, waking up to the Self. Why should the Self still be looking? Look around. It is still looking, still inquiring. Still realizing itself in every possible way, in spite of Buddha, Jesus, Ramana and all those big guys, but they all said it in a way – "Existence is and nothing but existence is". And you are That, so be it. That is your nature and that you cannot not be. Enjoy yourself because this takes a while. What to do?

Pointers are only pointers. They cannot bring anything. So, no help. But that for me is the biggest help you can get. That nothing has to be given to you, nothing can be taught to you what you not already are. This paradox has to be there all the time. These pointers are not coming out of me, these pointers have already been made infinite times by infinite books, by Nisargadatta, by Ramana. They are always pointing and asking 'Can life be born?' If you could just drop this ownership, this mind, it will all be fine. It always was and always will be.

Q: I can't do anything about it...

K: The ownership drops when it drops. It doesn't even have to drop, that's the problem. Even that dropping would be one dropping too much. Let drop what can drop. [Pointing to a visitor] Did you drop?

Q: I have no idea...

K: That's one idea too many; especially one who has no idea.

Q [Another visitor]: If there is nothing to do and nobody could be rescued from this state of dreaming, these words of Vishnu that destroys the illusion are they really part of the illusion? The Self does not need anything, so why does Self enjoy listening to itself?

K: That is the joy. That is the nature of entertainment, that there is an entertainment without you needing it. If you would need it, it would not be entertaining, it would be work.

Q: So, this is Self entertaining itself?

K: This is Self entertaining itself but not needing it. But it cannot help itself. It has to entertain itself because there is no other way. If it wakes up, it has to entertain itself, it cannot stay as a potential. It cannot stay there because there is no one who wants anything. It cannot avoid waking up. And there entertainment starts because you have to be awake to want not to be awake. It is always too late. Entertainment started, so now be entertained by what-you-are. The divine accident happened. But did something happen by that, that's the problem. Entertainment started, so now be entertained by what-you-are. You cannot stop it anymore. You cannot get rid of it anymore because you started this business.

Now, being stupid enough to avoid your business and wanting to get out of this business, you are in trouble. It makes you very busy. That is part of the business, trying to get out of the business. Everyone knows that if you have a running business, to get out of it is very hard. Whatever you do is too late now. Just see that it is too late. That was the main point of Buddha that the divine accident happened. The divine accident that your Absolute Buddha nature woke up. It woke up to being aware of its existence and out of the existence comes 'I Amness', the conscious, and out of that comes the unconscious. The aware, conscious and unconscious – the trinity comes, just by entertainment. When the Absolute wakes up, it has to wake up to the absolute possibility of every possible experiencing. So, it happened!

But did really something happen for what-you-are? No. You are still that which is potential what-you-are, as you were prior to waking up and you will be beyond waking up. That is the meaning of being prior, with and without whatever you can imagine. But you started to imagine yourself. You started to imagine yourself by imagination, but by none of the imagination you can gain what-you-are, since you haven't lost yourself in the first place. But now you are trapped in your own imagination and you think by another imagination you can get out of it. Impossible! You cannot get out of where you are not in... that's the main problem. If you really were in, consciousness is clever enough and there would be a way out. The absolute intelligence of Consciousness would find a way out if there would be someone in the prison. Don't undermine the absolute existence of consciousness.

But the problem is there is no one in, who could get out. So, you try the most intelligent understanding. It is wonderful, but it doesn't help because the main problem is there is no one who needs to be helped. But you try. So, you become a Mick Jagger again and again – "I can't get no satisfaction". There is a *neti-neti* in that – because I am already satisfied. Even Mick Jagger is a self-made puppet who is singing the song of the Self. Do you think Mick Jagger invented anything? It is all the song of Self singing for itself.

[Interruption]

Where was I? You always have to recollect where was 'I'? Without that recollection there is no 'I', there is not even an idea of the cluster. It needs attention to be collected. Normally you look out of the window and no one looks.

Q [Another visitor]: What kind of energy do you feel at this place? To me it feels similar to be being in Tiruvannamalai...

K: It is a timeless energy here.

Q: When we came to this place, I lost the sense of time. It is like being in a black room and not knowing where is the world around me and I don't know where is my brain...

K: The limits are less here. Your body consciousness stretches out in the place.

Q: Yesterday when someone was talking to me, I was not able to answer; I was not able to make a connection with her...

K: That is what Maharaj meant when he said once I was born and took the idea of the body as real. After the 'Who Am I' by realizing the 'I Amness', I became space-like and unlimited in my nature. You get out of the tunnel view of the 'me', the story, to the impersonal stretching out into the infinite. Maybe this energy is helping for that experience. There are always energy places or power places that can help you for that. Helping you to step out of the tunnel view of the 'I' into the bodiless space of an unpronounced 'I Amness' – the identified and the non-identified. Then you don't know where your limits are anymore. Then you don't know what is thinking, then the space is thinking, the space is acting. But there is no 'me' anymore which is the creator. The impersonal doing happens. Then you have to just recollect and make a past and future again. You even need a little effort to get into the past and future again. So, it is a nice place and for that it may help.

Then there are other places like Arunachala where you go a bit further, into the Light which is the source of the 'I Amness', of the identified and the non-identified. And then it ends. It is always like from the tunnel, the open and that what is the tunnel and the open, the superior 'I', the awareness which is sometimes closed and sometimes open. And these are the two ways – definer defining itself, or the collector collecting or not collecting memories. In the collecting memories there is a story, and in not collecting memories, there is no story.

Q: When you speak, I remember only the last few words and they are gone again. When you need to collect them back, it needs an effort...

K: That's why we can talk about it as an entertainment because you cannot take it home. This you cannot take home, you cannot make it your understanding or your openness. That's the beauty of openness; it cannot be 'your' openness. The moment you want to recollect it, it's gone. The moment you want to memorize it, it's gone. Then you are in this tunnel again and then you worry again. So, what to do?

Q: It's just a little strange...

K: You will get used to it. [Laughter] That's what Ramana

means 'being in good company'. When you are in the company of openness, consciousness always adjusts to that. Then in this company, it becomes that openness. If you go to the company of awareness, it becomes the awareness; then you adjust to the awareness. Consciousness is just like an actor, it always takes over the role with which it is presented, with the presence that is there. When you are in the company of a stock broker, you are totally in the stock market. It just sucks you in. If you are in the company of monks, you are totally in different space. Be surprised. You can be manipulated by the circumstance totally. Wherever you are, circumstance dictates what you experience and how you experience. It's not your choice. Never! When you are in an ashram, you feel in different space than being in a military camp. The circumstance takes you over sometimes immediately and sometimes after some time... but you will be as your surroundings.

Q [Another visitor]: And if you live alone?

K: [Joking] Then you become Milarepa. We are caves here, you can sit in them. When are you ever alone?

Q: When I am alone in my room, what do I become? My Self?

K: You can never become your Self. That's the idea hermits have when they go to caves. They think when no one is around me anymore, I become that space. I would not be disturbed anymore, I get out of the tunnel view of my story. In Castaneda and Shamanism it is the same. Recollect and get rid of the personal story, then stepping into the impersonal story. That's everywhere; always trying to control. Always thinking that this is wrong and is bothering me so I want to have a release from this. What then? Always thinking, that is better than this.

Q: I was wondering what happens when I am alone...

K: Just do it and we will see. You will long for the company again that you miss. Then you would think the company was not so bad, I am bored with myself here. At least there I have something to do, talk about something. That's the idea about everyone who goes to the cave thinks that when I am alone, I become myself because that is a good circumstance for my so-called spiritual progress. There are so many books written about that, getting siddhis. Fantastic! But I tell you, it is not any more entertaining than having a sip of coffee. There is nothing wrong with that, but for sure it is not better than having a sip of coffee.

But we can talk about it, that it is all possible. But by all of that, you cannot attain what-you-are, that's the beauty of it. So, it has the same quality as sitting in a cave for fifty years and developing all the siddhis and whatever you can imagine. You become the Avatar of the universe. It is the same control mechanism and you are still the same fucking bastard that you are now.

Q: I am glad to hear that because whenever I meditated, I was waiting for it to get over. I never liked it...

K: No one likes it. You think people like to meditate?

Q: [Laughing] My husband liked it...

K: Because of that he died so early. [Laughter] He meditated and closed his eyes while driving.

Q [Another visitor]: Can you talk about spirits that are around constantly seeking attention?

K: [Pointing to the people] Look at all the spirits here around. What about those spirits? They are the same, not any different. Spirit in body and spirit in no-body is no different. Consciousness doesn't need a form, come on!

Q: But they seek attention out of play?

K: For them they are as real as you think yourself to be. It makes no difference. For them, maybe you are the ghost. [Laughter] If death happens suddenly, they are out and they don't even imagine that they are dead. They feel they are still there and they want to talk to people but no one sees them anymore. Then they have to find other ways to get attention. All happens in that dream-like whatever... Everything is possible, why not? But what to do with it? Enjoy it!

Q: I was in a room where the energy felt really uncomfortable...

K: Take it like Milarepa. He had to sing a song. Just start singing, entertain them. And in the entertainment, they melt away, as you melt away. I have no idea. Nothing has to happen. If you don't like the room, go somewhere else. You don't have to prove anything. There is no improvement or progress needed; that you have to embrace the spirits and put them in your heart and be full of compassion for them. Blah, blah, blah... If you don't like it, go somewhere else.

Q: So, it has to do with the place?

K: Sometimes they are around your neck. But who cares? They are always following you because you are entertaining for them, as you give attention to them. If there is someone who doesn't care, they would go to someone who cares. And you care! [Laughter] You care that you don't want them. Little cats come only to the people who don't want them. Cats always come to people who have allergy. If you feel that you don't want them, they like you. Because not wanting is like love. It's like "He doesn't give attention to me because he doesn't like me". You don't go to people who don't care about you. Caring or not-caring, liking or not-liking is fine. You don't go to any place where no one cares about you. It's like the spirits; they go to people who care about them by not wanting them. So, what about the caretaker?

It needs two to tango. It needs one to dance and another one who wants or doesn't want to dance.

Q: I just need to get used to it...

K: Why should you get used to it? Just enjoy it. The absolute control is controllessness. When you are what-you-are, which is that Existence, there is no higher energy than that. And helplessness is the highest energy because helplessness is the nature of the Almighty. And there is no spirit around you, you are That. There is an entity outside or inside. You already have so many entities inside. A little bit more or less, who cares? You are already schizophrenic inside and there are so many entities like a cluster. Who cares about a little bit more ghost-like identities who want to have fun?

Spirit is obsessed by Spirit; it is playing all the roles. Consciousness plays all the roles of being an entity and beings and then it says, 'Oh this being I don't like'. Consciousness plays all the roles, the spirit and the one who likes it or doesn't like it. And what happened? Nothing happened. There is always that bastard you are who enjoys everything, come on! Enjoy the stupidity because you are stupid enough to believe in yourself. And by believing in yourself, you left what-you-are. So what happens now? You became a believer and now you believe that you exist and then you believe in others. A believer is one who left what-he-is because he is a leaf of existence but not the existence anymore. He believes in being, but doubts it permanently. Then, in the fear of doubting, trying to control the surroundings. What to do?

Q [Another visitor]: Can you say that you don't have the tendency of controlling anything anymore?

K: No. I don't have any tendency of controlling the controlling. [Laughter] That's different. You have to control your steps to go to the toilet, even if it is automatic it seems like there is a control. It always 'seems like'; there was never any control of anything. It is all an automatic happening. It seems like an experience of controlling but there was never any controlling.

Q: You don't have any suffering linked to that?

K: No. I cannot suffer about what I am. Suffering is only in time and suffering can only happen when there is a second. There are all kinds of experiences but there is no suffering in it; never was, never will be. Suffering only happens when the Almighty steps out of his nature imagining that there is one. When there is one, there is a second and then there is suffering. As you are what-is, how can you suffer about that? Suffering needs two or one, because even one is too many. So, we are talking about the end of a sufferer, which is the end of suffering. We are not talking about the end of suffering or controlling, we are talking about the end of controller. And the worst for the controller is that no one needs it to go. This is the coolest fire of carelessness, that no one can survive.

Only when you are what-you-are, there is carelessness which is the coolest fire of all. It burns down the hell. But no other fire can burn it down. They call it the fire of heart, to be that existence which is Heart itself; that which has no heart. It burns down all that can be burnt. Only when you are that what is grace, even dropping the idea of grace, being that what-is. But this cannot be done, this cannot be taught, this cannot be given, nothing can be done about that. No one can be it for you and don't care about anyone who can or cannot. That would be really stupid. Care only about what-you-are and not if anyone else is realized or not realized, enlightened or not enlightened. All that is second-hand. Be totally selfish about that what-you-are. It doesn't help but...

Q: It does, in a way...

K: Whatever you do is you want to end suffering. Whatever comes out of the relative 'I' always tries to end suffering. Every action of consciousness is an action towards happiness. Every self-inquiry is inquiring into happiness because you want to end suffering and you really think that by controlling it, you can end it. You imprison yourself in that idea. Even not to control, is control. In one instant you see that there is no way out of it and then the controller drops. But not because something special happened. It is in spite of what happened before. It is like 'Ah', and nothing happens in that.

The worst for the 'I' or intellect is that nothing has to happen. Nothing has to be changed for that. In that it burns down and sooner or later it would be gone in that. You may say that there is a progress or process of that. It feels like a running out energy and one day it is totally gone and you don't even realize it, because there was nothing before. So, by-the-way it is gone. So, it is nothing special. It is not a firework of enlightenment experiencing the deepest insight of your nature; pure energy spreading all over the place; energy balls penetrating all around. Blah, blah, blah...

It is your very nature and it was always there. It was never-never and never had any before or after. So, it is absolutely nothing special. It is here-now what-you-are and it will never be different in its nature. It never demanded anything, never needed anything, it is always the fulfilment itself, satisfaction itself. It is the very *Sat* and *Sat* cannot be hungry for *Sat*. So, it is the nature of satisfaction and that what is the nature of Sat was never-never. That what you call spirit or phantom 'I' will always be hungry. There is no way out of the spirit being hungry for the next sensation and always imagining that the next will be better because that's what keeps the universe going on – the greed of consciousness wanting to know consciousness. This is biting the apple in paradise. It bit into the apple and then all the answers were there; I Am was there as paradise, the unpronounced. From there comes, what? By the absolute question 'What', there are all absolute answers. For the absolute question 'What?', these are all the absolute answers. But you cannot see all the answers together; you can only see fragments of answers. That's the problem. You are not satisfied by fragments as you don't see the entire answer at once. So, you better go back to the questioner.

There is the question 'Who Am I?' and then there is fulfilment. 'Who' drops, 'Am' drops, 'I' drops and you are left as the Absolute leftover, which can never not be That what is the Absolute leftover Itself. You always will be the Absolute answer of the question 'Who Am I?' – Silence. That is the famous meditation of 'Who Am I'. But you cannot say by that meditation, you attain yourself. It is simply what can drop drops in front of you and you still are what-you-are. So, it is not something new, there never was something old. There was always this pre-sense, this in-no-sense(innocence) of what-you-are. Everything drops and you are still it. That is Ramana's death experience – the form, the formless, the awareness of the light dropped and still he was that what is Life; Life itself totally without any experience – That what you cannot not be. That you are here-now, that you may call the Absolute Seer, because without the Absolute Seer, there is no seer, no seeing, nothing can be seen. The seer you can see is already part of the scenery. But it needs the Absolute Seer that there can be a seer, seeing, what can be seen.

Without the pre-sense, there is no presence of whatever you can imagine. Realize yourself as That and there was never any problem at all; never was, never will be. And That never has any hunger for anything. There is Self-satisfaction Itself which was always there, it is never anything new. You simply gave your attention to something in front of you, but nothing happened. So, even giving attention to the form, the formless, makes no difference. All the differences are there, but they cannot make any difference for what-you-are. So, what to do? The next will be the next; and then, and then, and then... never-ending story. You step out of the relative story into the absolute story; that's all. Out of a relative owner, to the absolute owner because you are the absolute owner of whatever is and is not. This is the only thing that happens. You step out of the jiva into the Shiva, out of the knowing into the absolute not-knowing, because this is the absence of one who knows or doesn't know what one is.

But you don't step out of it. You were never in that's the problem. You experience yourself as if you had stepped out. There was an experience that you stepped in, there is a forgetting. Then there is remembering: in remembering it drops in front of you. It seems like by remembering something, you become something, but you don't even become something. There is an experience of becoming, but there is no one who became it.

So, I don't deny experiences and process. There was a process of going out and there's a process of going back. But by the experience of going out, what-you-are didn't go out. So, by the experience of going back, you don't go back. But still, both are there. The dream was that you went out and in the dream you go back. But actually in the dream, no one went out, and in the dream no one went home. There is only a possibility of forgetting because you are; there is a possibility of remembering because You are. And that was uninterrupted – never more or less. That's the quality of your nature which is never more or less as it is. The more or less is an imaginary dream in front of you. But in the more or less, the quality has nothing to gain... and again and again you are That what has nothing to gain.

Knowing the spirits and what this place is doing or not, it's entertainment. Controlling or not controlling, you can only control yourself. But no one is controlled. Consciousness controlling consciousness is still consciousness. Nothing happens. Freedom imprisoned by freedom is still freedom. That's the freedom of the second. To be that which is the Self being imprisoned by the Self, nothing is there. Freedom is imprisoned by freedom, so what? My goodness. Peace is in peace; shanti, shanti, shanti.

Q [Another visitor]: Earlier I thought 'I Amness' is the bridge, but now it seems there is no bridge...

K: There cannot be a bridge. It is like everything collapses, but there is no bridge. It drops away but by seeing it as it is. But nothing drops. You expect something to drop. But the dropping is not that something drops. You step from the form to non-form, to formlessness and even to the prior. This is an experience, but nothing happened by that because you were already prior and beyond that what you think you are. But still there is an experience. You went out by the experience that you were born into the gross body. But did your nature change by that?

Then you go to the meditation of Oneness, unpronounced 'I Amness' – wonderful! Then you see it is not even that! Then the 'I Amness' drops and the pure light of 'I' remains as Samadhi of light. Then in one instant, you see that even the light that you experience cannot be what-you-are and then even the light drops. But it is still there. The dropping is that you cannot see what-you-are and whatever you see cannot be that. Even the seer, which is the purest awareness, the notion of 'I' as awareness, you can experience. But what you can experience, you cannot be. Prior to that purest notion of 'I', has to be that what is the Absolute experiencer. The Absolute experiencer is always in spite of any experience.

In spite of form, in spite of formless, in spite of 'I', you are That Brahman, Atma and everything is all there – as an experience. And they are not different from what-you-are but are not That. Don't understand it, don't even try. [Laughter] Because the understanding you have now will drop anyway. It will be gone in the next five minutes.

Q: The fear that arises again and again...

K: It will never stop. Why should it stop? For who? You really think Existence is in need to not fear to be what is existence? You really think Existence itself needs absence of fear to be? What kind of bullshit existence would it be who doesn't have to fear to be what-it-is? What kind of bullshit rubbish existence would it be that depends on the absence of fear? You are with and without – that's all. Who cares about the presence or absence of anything? And whose fear is it anyway?

But it is love; you care about yourself so very much. This loving business, the lover cares about the beloved. Then one moment it starts hating that it loves it. God falls in love with God; poor God. Then being in the self-pity of love because out of love it falls into the self-pity of love. Now he hates to love himself. Now he wants to get out of that love affair because this love affair is not fulfilling the Promised Land because the loved became the hated.

Now he becomes a meditator, a seeker who wants to kill oneself. You are after that; you want to kill yourself because you are fed up with yourself. I want to be nothing now. You think, 'If I would be nothing, I would be better off'. The 'me' again. So, love is maybe not so good. Maybe you want to think about it because for love it needs two. So, you better be that Heart which has no heart. That what can have a heart, needs a churchury(surgery) of heart-opening. What bullshit open-heart would it be? What heart needs to be an open heart to be that what is Heart? Only a relative one, an imaginary heart. An imaginary open heart. Then you run around looking at people, is your heart still closed? Mine is so open. [Laughter] I can help you. Wonderful!

Then they call themselves Heart Masters... they mastered their heart. Sounds very nice. Poor heart! Poor heart has a master now. Walking, running, compassion; an open heart. Then making everyone else jealous. [Mocking] You can have it too, if you just follow my steps. Be in the presence of me and you will have an open heart as well. [Laughter] Isn't it nice how consciousness plays the master and the slave? Playing both roles perfectly till the end; the disciple and the master. The one and only Oscar of all time goes to... Consciousness. The winner again is... Consciousness. [Laughter] Today it comes as Jack Nicolson, but again, it is Consciousness. The winner of all time and the loser of all time in the ok and ko business of boxing itself – Consciousness, in the ring of consciousness. So, even as a winner you have nothing to lose, or as a loser you have nothing to win, or is it the opposite? I cannot remember. [Laughing]

That is the famous, 'nothing ever happened'. Consciousness plays and plays and plays in the roulette. Sometimes there is Auro-bingo! [Laughter] The one who got all the numbers right. Then there is one with the lottery – I am now enlightened. All the numbers are right. Then one walks around; everything is perfect. Bingo!! [Laughter] Thank God no one ever reached anything. Isn't it fun?

I am not here to make anyone feel comfortable; for sure not. If at all, maybe the opposite. I am here to make you absolutely uncomfortable, that you may experience total chaos and still you are what-you-are. And That what-you-are never needs any comfort to be what-it-is, that is the Absolute comfort. So, take absolute comfort in that what never needs to be in any comfort at all. That what needs to be in the comfortable circumstance and needs to have a comfort; oh my goodness! If really existence would require comfort, what kind of bullshit existence would it be? A relative one and not worth being.

You are in comfort and in discomfort That what-you-are. The comfortable experience and the uncomfortable existence doesn't make you more or less as you are. Take comfort in that where no one needs to be in comfort. But that what you call your so-called relative body-mind organism always needs and always tries to be in comfort. Even by being a masochist you think that by being a masochist you'll be in the comfort of 'I-lessness' or ego-lessness. Every sexual activity is for that, getting away from oneself. There 'I' was not and now I want to have it again. I again want to have that what I am not, where both are gone. Then both came back. [Laughter] What a drive in that tendency! You have an orgastic experience with someone and then you are glued to that experience. You want to have it again and again. Then you even marry to have it again and again but it never happened again. But you are still waiting for it. Maybe it happens again, and then it's even worse. [Laughter]

This is the glue – you are glued by love. You are glued by that glue which is called love; your loving-caring glue by which you are glued to the relative existence you think you are. What a glue! And you have a clue. Because you have a clue, you are glued to that glimpse.

Q [Another visitor]: It is hard for women to hear what you say...

K: And for men too.

Q: Women approach it differently. You are breaking the love...

K: As I said, love has to be broken so that love can be what is love that doesn't know love.

Q: I understand it in theory but in the feeling level it is difficult to hear that...

K: It's hell. And I'm here to produce hell. As I said, I'm not here to make anyone comfortable.

Q: I can see that...

K: [Laughing] This is that carelessness that you may call love; but it doesn't know love. That what is Shiva destroys all relative love that can be there so that love can be that again what is Love or heart can be again that what is Heart that has no heart. Your idea of love or heart depends on things called 'my'. My heart, my feelings, my love. That is the glue. You are glued to the lover loving his beloved body or existence. This relative love is suffering, never was, never will be. There is a temporary release of something and then immediately back again.

Only that what is Heart can... but not this relative ownership heart-knot, a possessed heart where an owner is involved. It is like a possession. You are possessed by the idea that you can know yourself. There is an owner of heart, 'my' heart, 'my' existence. That is your reality and it is a fake one, and out of that falsity, you suffer.

How to get rid of that falsity? Not by making you comfortable or sweet-talking of love, about loving heart and bullshit. All that bloody loving heart has to go in a way. It has to drop as an idea. You have to see that by none of that you can be happy, thank God. And you have to enjoy that none of that relative loving bullshit can make you happy. It's fun, it's entertainment. But by that entertainment you cannot enter yourself. So, thank God it's worth nothing. All the precious relative 'me' loving someone and the feelings and the intuition, thank God they are worth nothing. Not a dime. They are just shit in nature because they cannot bring you the chit of what-you-are.

That is fun, hitting all these icons. There would be a perfect master, there would be a perfect moment or understanding, once upon a time... this fairy tale will continue forever and you will bite into the tail of the fairytale forever. [Laughter] Then you would say that it hurts again and again. I thought it was a fairytale; I just bit into my tail. Oh it's me. Shit! [Laughter]

Have fun about sex and relationship, who bloody cares? But thinking that by all the tantra business you can attain what-you-are is again suffering, because it makes you depending on action or non-action or being in tune with someone or not. What an idea!

Q [Another visitor]: Papaji would say, whatever we do physically is for the physical, whatever we do mentally is for the mental, whatever you do spiritually is for the spirit. But it has absolutely nothing to do with what-you-are...

K: Thank God. Let the mind fuck what the mind can fuck. It's a mind-fuck anyway. Let the mind have sex and orgasm as much as it likes, who cares? So, it's all in a way mind-fuck.

Q: Thinking that I can get something out of this is suffering. Action happens but wanting to get more out of it or not wanting the action is suffering...

K: Love. I am not joking, love is suffering! Whatever idea of love, it makes you suffer. No way out. In love there is passion and passion is suffering. Passionate love. But what to do?

Q [Another visitor]: What about compassionate love?

K: There is no compassionate love. Compassion knows no love. Compassion is your nature and compassion doesn't know anyone else. Compassion is Grace itself and there is no love in it. No lover and no beloved and no second. Compassion is the nature of existence and in compassion there is no love because there is no one who could love. There is no lover and no beloved. There is no two.

Q: So, as soon as we have a lover and a beloved, we are in trouble?

K: Absolutely. Any moment you are the lover and you are separate from your beloved, you are in trouble.

Q [Another visitor]: What about unconditional love?

K: When there is unconditional love, it creates conditional love. It creates hell again.

Q: Why does it have to be created?

K: Because the unconditional love means 'I Amness', the unpronounced. Then out of the unpronounced, comes the pronounced. The root thought of the pronounced is the unpronounced. Both come together, so even the unpronounced is the potential of suffering.

Q [Another visitor]: If we already have so many personalities inside of us, why not include someone else?

K: What someone else? Any second is hell.

Q: But there is already second...

K: There is no second. There was never any second, that's the problem. But by your bloody imagination you create a second 'you' and someone else, then the hell starts.

Q: That's just in the nature of personality...

K: There is no nature of a personality. Fuck the personality bullshit.

Q: You mentioned that before...

K: I said the cluster of energy which is the identified consciousness that you call as 'me', not less, not more! The cluster is what you call as a personal story. The collection of memory effects from the past and future expectations that you call the cluster of energy which is the 'me' which wakes up in the morning and collapses at night. But you take yourself as that... come on!

Q: How is that different to having a relationship?

K: There is no one who has a relationship. There is one cluster and another cluster. There is energy but there is no relation. There is an action and reaction of action of consciousness. There is no one who has a relationship with anything. Consciousness cannot have relationship with another consciousness. There is no second-edition of consciousness, my goodness! So, there is no relationship possible; never was, never will be! Having another person inside is a relationship – bullshit. Every kind of relating to something is hell. That's why it is called re-late, it's too late! You re-late. You're reloaded into bullshit.

Q [Another visitor]: So, it is a different kind of energy interaction?

K: There is energy in a different information. There are two informations interacting, but both in essence, is energy. There is no relationship. It is a dream of a movie of relationship; Hollywood unlimited. And if you walk the holy-wood way, you can walk forever. [Laughter] It's an infinite movie of relationships but there is no one who has one, that's the main thing. So, why bother? Enjoy all that bullshit but don't think something comes out of it. And don't call it your bullshit – 'my' relationship. That makes you depending, that makes you imprisoned by that. My bloody relation and my being in tune and God Almighty. It's my tea, not your tea. The all-my-tea God!

Q [Another visitor]: Doesn't life come out of the relationship?

K: Absolutely not. How can life come out of bullshit? How can life come out of anything anyway? How can life be born from whatever? Can life be born in something? What bullshit life can be born? That bullshit life which can be born is already dead. Life cannot be born, come on. Buddhists have a nice picture. Two lovers making love and a little baby comes out. When you see that picture from another perspective, you see two skeletons creating another skeleton. That's all. Out of dead, only dead comes. Out of dead phenomenal experiences, only dead phenomenal experiences come out. They are all empty. Life is never born. How can life come out of life? In life nothing happens, come on! You really think this is life? This permanently changing phenomenal experiences. Come on! How can life be born? The very idea of birth is death. Out of two dead lovers comes another dead lover.

[Pointing to visitors] Look, mother and daughter sitting there. [Laughter] But this is the realization of Mary. This is the symbol of Virgin Mary. The mother who saw her son being crucified and seeing there was never any son who was crucified. And she was never a mother of anyone. And she was never a child of any mother. That was the realization of Mary. That's why in south America Mary is considered to be higher than Jesus.

The love of a mother, seeing that there is no son being crucified. There is consciousness and nothing can happen to Life. And she being alive never came out of any mother. This is the realization of Mary. That is the biggest symbol of Christianity. For me, she is higher than Jesus in that way. A mother seeing that there is no son being crucified. Then enjoying that realization. Can you do that?

But that is what you are here for. To be a child of a barren woman which in essence is unborn and never dying, Absolute Self. And that never gave birth to anything. That you are not mother of a daughter. That this is a dream realization experience but no one has that. And to see in your daughter, That what-you-are – Absolute unconditioned existence. Cosmic consciousness looking into cosmic consciousness and not being anyone's mother and not being anyone's daughter. Never born, never died.

That is what you are here for... to release the bloody imagination, because that idea is only a memory, a fairytale of being a mother. Once upon a time, something came out of this body experience. Then you call it love because it is yours. The owner becomes a lover loving whatever he owns. You love what came out of your body because it is closer to you than what came out of other bodies. That's what we call the ownership love, what came out of 'my' precious. It is like the Lord Of The Rings – 'my precious'.

That is the best symbol of you cannot drop your precious. Even the purest heart, Frodo stood there and could not drop it. He wanted to go back and keep it. Then the turbulence of the circumstance made the drop but not by him wanting it. He could not do it. It will drop, but not by your action. You can never give up your beloved. Never!

The beloved is the idea that one day you can know yourself. That is like the Lord Of The Rings; that you can control existence. You cannot give up this consciousness, it gives up by itself, in spite of your wanting it or not – never because. But we can only talk about the beginning of the suffering. And the beginning of suffering is that you become the owner of existence. The owner of existence falling in love with his belongings – with himself. And that falling in love, you cannot avoid as you could not avoid sitting here.

Now we talk that out of love trying to attain what-you-are, that is an illusion. That is an imagination. That it continues, it makes no difference. But the imagination that something comes out of it, that you can attain something by the action or non-action... that's prison, that's slavery. And in slavery, you suffer about being the slave of love. So, even the love makes you a slave. Then you have a master who gives you a new name as Slave Of Love. Then you are proud of that bloody name because you are so much in love with the name of love. It becomes such an icon because everyone around you talks about love and there are movies about eternal love and unconditional love. Then you're melting away in your heart and then you are tear-jerking around love, again and again. That's why these movies from Hollywood are tear-jerking movies. And they always catch you again and again because they exactly know where to put you.

So, it is all like devil's advocate talking to you – Mephisto. Mephisto always wants to tempt you, promising you that something comes out of this. Sometimes it appears as love and sometimes it appears as wisdom. Always tempting you, always telling you if you follow me I can give you the promised because by me you can gain or attain what-you-are. Then you can know yourself and you will have full control. All the empty promises. Thank God.

Q: Osho told me first you will be slave of love and then you will become master of love...

K: Look at her all empty promises. The devil himself promised her bloody name. [Mocking] He promised me, he waits for me, he left me his dream. Wonderful! I like Osho but only because he is dead. [Laughter]

Q: Never born, never died... [Laughter]

K: Normally when they ask me what do you think about my former guru Osho? At that moment I tell them that as Osho I was not so bad either. At that moment, Osho is gone. Suddenly there is no Osho anymore; there is just consciousness that played Osho. Once there was Osho now there is no-show.

Q: He also said freedom is higher than love. So I can't be so proud...

K: Now you are proud that you are not proud. [Laughter]

Q [Another visitor]: This unconditional love...

K: Unconditional love is already 'I Amness'. I have to say it is still a concept.

Q: Imagine that there is someone who is realized...

K: That is like imagining hell. [Laughter] Imagine there is one who is or could be realized, both is hell.

Q: What remains of Karl here [Pointing to Karl]...

K: It's not so bad.

Q: When you look at us as you are looking at Self, that's unconditional love...

K: No. There is no Self. [Laughter] I cannot see myself in anyone. How can I see myself in you? That would be two, one sees and the other one is seen. You talk about the oneness love, that you can reach.

Q: So, why do you say it is impossible for a couple?

K: How can there be two in oneness? So, there is no couple.

Q: And then...

K: There is no then. There never was any couple. So what? There is no oneness because oneness needs two. Oneness is the source of separation. That's why I say oneness which is heaven creates hell. The unconditioned love creates conditioned love.

Q: So, we cannot talk about oneness?

K: Of course we can talk about it. In every peak point of oneness, you are in orgasm with your beloved. Sufi's try that all the time, merging into God. It is oneness in which the subject-object disappears.

Q. When there is oneness there is no judgment...

K: You think oneness can be destroyed by judgment. What kind of bullshit oneness would it be?

Q: Of course not...

K: So why not judge? [Laughter] When there is judgment there is still oneness.

Q: There is more peace...

K: Who needs more quantity of peace?

Q: I, I, I...

K: I know. But who cares about your greedy 'I'? Not me.

Q: I do care...

K: Care as much as you like. No one cares that you care.

Q: But I care...

K: It's enough that you care. Don't make anyone else care about it.

Q: It helps me...

K: That's selfish. I only talk about my love because it helps me.

Q: It helps others as well...

K: [Asking a visitor] Does it help you?

Q [Another visitor]: No...

K: You see. [Laughter]

Q: It does help...

K: It doesn't help talking about relationship then working on relationship. Then they split again and you say 'I worked so much on you and now you are leaving me. I made you as I like you and now you are leaving me. All for nothing. I worked so hard, no stinking socks anymore and you behaved as I liked and now you are leaving me, shit.'

Q: But that's okay too, let's see...

K: I don't like to wait and see. I am not a waiter. Shall we wait now?

Q [Another visitor]: And what do you like?

K: Just 'see' not 'wait and see'.

Q: We see but we keep forgetting, it's not our fault...

K: Of course it is your fault.

Q: I am blaming myself...

K: You can blame yourself but that's stupid.

Q: I know it's stupid but it still happens...

K: That's why I say, the only thing I can find is the unlimited stupidity of what I Am. And who cares? And the absolute unlimited stupidity cannot make me more or less as I Am. So, it is fun. But I cannot find knowledge and Thank God knowledge cannot be found in anything. Whatever you can find, whatever you cannot find out or understand is ignorance.

Q: Then I start to believe that and it becomes a concept too...

K: So what? Who cares if it's a concept or not? Now you make a concept that you don't want a concept. That makes you a concept. Concept or no-concept, who cares about a concept? You care about a concept and by that you become a concept.

Q: So, basically you are trying to cut down the victim here. You are doing a therapists role as well...

K: Why not? I chop whatever looks out.

Q: Removing all concepts is like cutting off the victim...

K: I shoot every duck that appears. It's like you are in a fair and you see the game where ducks pop up and then you shoot everything that pops up. Then you are very good in shooting and you shoot all the ducks down. Then you are very proud that I killed all the concepts. Then you see all the ducks popping back again. [Laughter] So, who cares about concepts or not? You shoot them out of fun or sport by knowing that they would pop up again. So, what?

Absolutely irrelevant talking and shooting. You even know that out of that destruction, the ducks would pop up again like phoenix out of the ashes... again and again and again. Wonderful! So, I have fun of shooting but do not expect that the concepts would be gone by that. Thank God. They would always pop up again. So what? Then you see whatever you shoot, pops up again. You cannot kill what's not there. You cannot kill what is already an image; as much as you try. But you cannot not try.

So, you try without expecting that something would come out of that shooting. And you shoot again and again like an inexhaustible machine gun. You don't even have to look anymore. You shoot everything with closed eyes, it doesn't matter. [Laughter]

Q: And we are idiots just enjoying the show...

K: If you take yourself as an idiot, you are self guilty. We are enjoying that nothing can be done or not done. So, you do or not do, who cares? That is joy. That is the nature of enjoyment, action without expectation of results.

Q [Another visitor]: We believe in these concepts of love and wisdom believing that they would bring us closer to ourselves. That is suffering...

K: That is the basis of suffering.

Q: I realize that I am so tired of seeking and that's why I suffer...

K: Seeking is not a problem. Trying to stop the seeking, you become a sufferer of seeking. Seeking by itself is automatic. It's like Ramesh when he was translating; he realized that the translation was happening automatically without his involvement. There is no more to it. Everything is an automatic action out of consciousness or whatever you call it, but it is automatic. What-you-are is never involved in anything.

Q: Involvement is when I want more of it or don't want it...

K: When you have an interest in it, then it starts. When you put something in bank and want to have an interest out of it. It's like meditation becomes a bank. Then you put your interest, pay your attention. Then by paying attention, you want to have an interest out of it. Then you are in a little bit of a problem.

Q: Positive or negative?

K: Whatever. Positive or negative interest both is need. That makes you needy. There is a very subtle necessity of attention. That necessity can only be of the spirit or the phantom because what-you-are never needs any attention to be what-it-is. Only the phantom 'I' permanently needs the attention, it doesn't matter if it's negative or positive. Negative or positive love doesn't matter. Hate is the same. It is just one side of the coin of attention. The spirit the ghost-like 'I' always needs attention. It doesn't matter if it's negative or positive. If the positive doesn't work, you behave so bad that you get the negative attention. But you always need attention.

Q: Wisdom is like the negative attention, it is pulling back. Love is positive giving out. But both of them seem to be the same.

K: Two tendencies coming out of the same 'I'. The tendency of wisdom is like wanting to get rid of oneself; like the wisdom of emptiness. And love is like embracing everything, like the unconditioned love of oneness. Both the tendencies come out of the same source because there is one with the two tendencies and then he fucks himself by those two tendencies. It needs a fucker with two tendencies of not wanting to be a fucker anymore and one who wants to fuck everything by oneness love. One who wants to fuck everything and one who doesn't wants to fuck anymore.

Q [Another visitor]: So, what is the difference?

K: It needs a fucker. Let the fucker fuck or not fuck, who gives a fuck? [Laughter]

Q [Another visitor]: Fucked if I know! [Laughter]

K: That's the Australian way. In Australia every second word is fuck, fucking good, fucking bad. [Laughter]

Q [Another visitor]: Is it the same truth and love that Nisargadatta was talking about?

K: Yeah. What he meant was that my existence never demands any wisdom or love, but they are there as phenomenal experiences. But who cares? They have nothing to offer for what I Am. I Am absolutely independent of presence or absence of love. Absolutely independent of the presence of wisdom. That is what I Am. Love and Wisdom both demand a presence of 'me'. Without 'me' there is no love and without 'me' there is no wisdom. But I don't demand them.

I am absolute in spite. They are there because of me, but I am not because of them. Your nature is never because. But the imagination of phenomenal experiences of wisdom and love is because of you, but you are not because of them. So you are absolute independent of both. They may be there or not, who cares? Your nature never demands anything and in your nature there is no necessity of love or wisdom or understanding to be what-it-is. That is happiness in nature or ananda or chit or knowledge which never has to know anything to be what-it-is.

But wisdom has to be known to exist. Love has to be known to exist. So, it depends on a knower. Even the knower is dependent on being a knower. But that what is knowledge doesn't need a knower to be what is knowledge. And that is what-you-are. So, knowledge doesn't need a knower to be what-it-is. But the knower needs knowledge to exist.

Q [Another visitor]: The phantom that always needs attention, you can't push it away because then it gets even worse...

K: Or I can have fun with it. Like now I hit it and you experience that nothing happens. It's like a rubber nail; you can hit it with hammer infinite times it always pops out again. It seems you got it down but it is always back – The return of the 'I'.

Q: You can't do anything with the 'I' that pops up...

K: I never said you should do anything. It can only be the 'I' itself who wants to do something. The thief that lives by your attention now becomes a policeman and thinks that now I take care about the thief. It's like now it becomes a meditator and tells you that now I would take care so that it doesn't bother you anymore. But it is the same thief that is living by your attention as before. It is just changing its face. First it is like the ego and now it is like, "I would take care of the ego". It's the same story.

It's the same story of even the consciousness because even consciousness lives by your attention. So, even consciousness becomes an idea. So, where is consciousness? It's just there when you imagine it but you are even without. You are prior to it or in spite. With and without consciousness, you are. 'Prior' and 'beyond' are simply pointers. It simply means that you are with and without but never because. Consciousness is because of you but you are not because of consciousness. Forms are because of you but you are not because of forms. Spirit is because of you but you are not because of the spirit. Awareness is because of you but you are not because of the awareness.

You are prior and beyond the first notion of existence... that Existence which is prior and beyond the first notion of existence. Prior and beyond all imagination, you are That which is imagining itself but can never imagine that what one is. So, whatever you imagine to be is not what-you-are. But there can only be an imagination of that what-you-are because you are imagining.

10th June 2007
Ladakh, India

Many Answers, Many Questions And Nothing Happens

Q: When you are not in suffering it is easy to see its illusory nature and when you are, it is difficult to see its illusory nature...

K: What to do? There are many techniques but none works.

Q: So, that's it?

K: And if you see no technique works, what to do? Suffering is only when you hope that something will end.

Q: So, this cannot be used as a technique to not suffer by allowing suffering to continue?

K: Who allows that? Do you really think that suffering asked you – 'May I suffer today?' Then the queen says, 'Yes you may continue'. And when the queen says, 'Today, I don't like it today', what then?

Whatever you do, the confirmation is always needed by the ghost-like sufferer. There are many esoteric techniques but I am not the right person to talk about it. There are so many psychotherapists who know better what to do. [Pointing to a visitor] She made her own therapy when she went to Holland and now has to do that. Getting from Bavarian suffering to Dutch suffering is quite something. Every nation has a different suffering. When you are a German, you suffer just by being a German. If you are Australian, you suffer by not having enough identity. Always different ways of suffering.

And as many different kinds of sufferings, there are different kinds of treatments. If only that would help anyway. If I would only know myself, only if I was not born. And it's never right! It's always different suffering. There is no world without suffering. There is no relative life without suffering. What to do with it? The experience of being relative is already painful. Even the slightest idea of existence is misery. You can make it less or more with the treatments. What you do is like cutting the tree, but it would always grow again. The root thought 'I' is not totally out-rooted and there would always be a sufferer. How to out-root the 'I' thought. Any ideas?

Q [Another visitor]: Enjoy suffering...

K: Sometimes you may even succeed, but sometimes not. There is always a limit of how strong the suffering is. There is a limit of acceptance and when that is crossed, you suffer again. Then you try harder to have a higher limit by having more acceptance; another treatment. Then that would again be crossed. Everyone has already tried that; to have a higher tolerance limit. Open your heart, reconnect to your heart, embrace everything, I celebrate everything – all the Osho techniques.

Q: You suffer because of fighting with your girlfriend...

K: No. Suffering is when you want to find and she says, who cares? [Laughter] What violence in relationships! When I see love-stories its always like – help me God! Nothing is more violent than love stories. When you see a nice action movie, everyone is smiling. So, we are back to the basic question, where does relationship start? And is there any relationship without a second? Where does this imaginary relationship with yourself start? When there is no one else, there is already you and yourself. Suffering starts when there is two; or even when there is one. When there is one, there is already suffering. Imagine! Already when there is one, one exists and by that doubtful existence there is a suffering about that doubtful 'I'.

Q: You talked about out-rooting the 'I'...

K: How to get rid of the phantom which is imaginary? How to look through the imaginary existence idea? The famous answer is 'Be prior'. Experience yourself as the first 'I' thought. But how to experience that? Every morning it happens. By waking up, there is one who woke up and every night it drops again. What to do with the ego?

Q: According to you it's like a rubber nail, you can do nothing with the ego...

K: Or you can do whatever you like and it doesn't matter.

Q: The main point for me is anything that I do, it is the ego doing it...

K: Was there an ego that did anything?

Q: Do you call the 'I' thought as ego?

K: Ego is the false impression that there is a second, that there's a separation. That's ego.

Q: The 'I' thought is different to the 'me'...

K: It already starts with the 'I' thought, the potential 'me' is already there.

Q: But that is not the ego?

K: Out of that comes the ego. Ego is like a cluster of memory effects of a 'me' which is then a personality.

Q: Is it different to the root 'I'?

K: It is not different because in the nature they are same. It's the same realization starting as an 'I' thought then becoming a 'me'. It's like a tree, first the root and then the be-leaf systems coming out of it. It's like a tree rooted in the 'I' thought of awareness. Then on the branches there are belief systems; the leaves. Then whatever you do, it grows even more. Then they ask how to get rid of that? Or is there a one who wants to get rid of something? That's more the question.

Already when you ask, 'How can I get rid of it?' you confirm one who needs to get rid of something to be what he is. This is the out-rooting; by not finding the one who needs it. That is 'Who cares?'. It's not that you succeed in out-rooting something. By not finding someone who needs the tree to go, then there may be a phantom or not, who cares? That's the worst for the ego that can happen that no one cares if there is one or not. As you are with and without the imaginary dream-like whatever...

So, by being what-you-are that doesn't need anything to come or to go, there is never any difference at all by presence or absence circumstance. This is out-rooting the idea of any dependency at all. So, even if you succeed in out-rooting of a tree, you depend on the out-rooting of the tree. So, the absolute out-rooting is that you are just what-you-cannot-not-be, which is That what-you-are. That which never needed any difference at all, to be what-it-is. That is the absolute out-rooting and that is the worst for the devil to happen, that no one cares if there is one or not, when or where, who cares at all?

That's why I like Nisargadatta's last sentences – Now with this body-mind organism, the last tendencies of the so-called guy called Nisargadatta are going away. But still no one cares. Simply pointing out that there was no one there who cared about the presence or the absence of the so-called guy called Nisargadatta; smoking or not-smoking, being or not-being a guru or anything. Now everything goes and still no one cares. As he said – I am with and without consciousness, what I am. But still I put garlands around my guru's pictures and no one needs to explain that. And why not?

Being what-you-are, nothing is more easy than that! It is a total effortlessness of existence, total ease which was always there. Again, I can only present the absolute way out, never a relative one. No control system will ever work, thank God. And imagine you could be controlled by an controlled system. Even to imagine that is hell! Even that you imagine that you can be known or controlled or you need something to go for you to be, what does that make you? You already become disgusting, discussing with other egos about how disgusting everyone is. How are you today? That is how it starts.

But you want techniques to increase your tolerance limit because then everyone likes you as you are a better person. Sounds good. But in nature its already very doubtful and painful suffering. And by whatever dependency you are missing what you are. In missing what you are there is an on-going misery of the controller trying to control himself. But what to do?

Q: So, where does the controller start?

K. Right away. It is the first awareness of 'I'.

Q: But if you go back to awareness...

K: That is the root of the controlling. You try to find what is running the control system. But what is the basis of controlling? Where does the controller start? When that what-you-are becomes aware to exist.

Q: You mean there is a potential?

K: No. I mean already there is a tendency. This is the main tendency – By waking up someone woke up. And that someone woke up to awareness is simply being aware to exist. There is a doubtful existence and out of that doubtful existence, a doubter is there. There is no doubting but still the doubtful existence is there. And out of the potential doubtful existence, it starts to doubt. Then it becomes a doubter and then what can be doubted coming out of the very first awareness – one becomes aware to exist. God becomes aware to exist, God knows itself in that way.

Q: But that can't be avoided...

K: It is not about avoidance. It is simply like going back and questioning, did someone wake up when the awareness starts? Is there someone already or no one wakes up? Does the nature of existence become aware of existence when something starts? Does your nature start in awareness?

Q: No...

K: Then who cares about awareness?

Q: Good point...

K: So the tendency is there that God wakes up to become aware then there are two Gods – God becomes aware of God. There is the root of ownership there – 'my' existence – simply by being aware to exist. This superior consciousness already is the root thought of 'I' and in that the potential suffering. Even when there is no suffering, and I agree that in awareness there is no suffering. But already in that there is a potential of suffering. And if you go by that tendency of becoming aware, and by that becoming 'one' who is aware, and then, by being one that which is unpronounced 'I Am', and from that, becoming one who defines itself. And by definition, you become separate to yourself, permanently. And separation is unbearable and suffering.

But when you try to change it, it's already too late. You try to make everything one. There is separation and you cannot bear it and you want to make everything one. You want to understand it and control it by your understanding. You want to enhance your tolerance and acceptance limits by understanding. But all that is too late and you are totally exhausted by that. So, it may not be the solution.

Q: In the awareness 'I Exist', is the existence there?

K: Yes. But again, does existence start with awareness? So, who cares if there is awareness or not?

Q: But in relative sense, it's there...

K: But who cares about the relative sense? Does That what you want to know, care about existence? It's already too late. When you are looking out, you are looking for something to do. And I am not the first one to say it. This was the famous 'divine accident' of Buddha. Simply stay where you are by being in awareness, don't go towards the first tendency. But who can do that?

Q: It's clear that there is no one who wakes up, only existence is there...

K: So who cares now about it? [Laughter]

Q: In truth, I don't care but since we are talking about it, there is one who cares to know about the finer details...

K: That's fun and nothing happens in it. This is called the inquiry without expectation that by that inquiry something may change. Then it's fun, that's inquiry without expectation. Then you ask when does ego start? When does the expectation start that out of the actions some results of knowing should happen? When does that start? Or is it already there? Sometimes from fun comes serious business. It's always different. Sometimes you are involved, sometimes not. Sometimes it reminds itself, sometimes not. Sometimes sooner, sometimes later. Always surprising, always unpredictable. And permanently you are the helplessness, there is no one who can control it. It's just an unfolding of whatever you call it.

That is 'what to do'. Then even 'out-rooting' becomes an idea. If you cannot get rid of it, that is the out-rooting. As you cannot get rid of that what-you-are, it will always be different, sometimes that, sometimes not. Even by saying there is nothing changes in all those changes, is what? It seems like you have to realize that. Can existence really be something that has to realize something to be that what is the existence? You can only say it's part of the dream.

Q: And that is the joke. When it goes out in time you realize that there was nothing to realize...

K: Even that is part of the dream. It's quite a trick – then I realize that I have nothing to realize. You have to be that what is uninterrupted that-what-it-is who is never surprised by that. That's why they call it a silence which is uninterrupted what-it-is and not which is involved in inquiry or non-inquiry. It doesn't even know itself. So, where is peace? In knowing, or not knowing or neither? Or peace is the absence of any idea of what-is and what-is-not peace? Does absolute existence mean that there is no one who knows or doesn't know to exist or not to exist? That is the uninterrupted nature of existence. So, be that what is your nature and for that nothing ever happened. All these pointers! And no one can be it for you. Not even you can be it. Imagine! Many answers, many questions and nothing happens.

Q [Another visitor]: What to do?

K: Do whatever you don't do.

Q [Another visitor]: What is different in satsang than when we sit with you in a restaurant? It feels there are more things happening in satsang...

K: When I eat, I am Karl.

Q: Is it our attention which is different?

K: Maybe. Normally the attention goes to the world, to the scenery. Here the attention goes more inwards. Satsang is an inner view and eating is an outer view – food for the soul and food for the body. One is more fine the other is more gross; it's always different. You may say satsang is the spirit turning the vision inwards to that what is the spirit. In the world, it turns the vision outside to that what is the movement. And in both senses, it tries to get happy. Getting happy by eating, by having a sensation outside and by satsang being happy by the inner vision. Two different ways of trying to be happy. If you ask me, in both you cannot find it; neither outside nor inside. Both is empty.

Q: But this seems full...

K: It's just two different kinds of experiences. You may call one is love or fullness and the other one is feeling hungry. Fulfilled or hungry, for both it needs one who is fulfilled or hungry. It always switches, sometimes full, sometimes hungry. In satsang you may say there is an eternal now because your attention doesn't go to the future, it is more energetically concentrated on that what is the attention. Then there is a stillness which is enjoyable. Then you go out and go astray again. But for both, it needs one.

For a while in that circumstance there is a stillness, a kind of happiness. Then you go out of the door and its back again. You become a monk when you sit here and when you go out you have a monkey mind. You always try to find the key for happiness.

Why don't you go out of satsangs?

Q: I can't help it...

K: And I tell you, it should be 24 by 7 by 365. And you are right, who can do that? But this is existence. Existence is 24 by 7 by 365. It's not a bit more or a bit less. That is what I call silence which is 24 by 7 by 365. It is never-never – never in satsang or not in satsang. It doesn't even know satsang. It doesn't even know itself. It doesn't know any inside or outside or going in and out or anything. It never moves at all.

That's why I say, everything comes back to this silence, the absolute experiencer never moves. Everything that is moving is dream-like. Sometimes India comes to you as what-you-are, sometimes Australia comes to you as what-you-are. But you never go to Australia. There is a movement of the body but in that movement, you don't move. You are neither here nor there. What-you-are has no place and all the places appear in you. But all of that cannot be done.

That is why it's called the split second. And even that split-second doesn't happen. It is not like something that comes over you, like a new experience. The heart breaks by itself.

Q: And yet you remember...

K: It is not something that you remember. You are just like – what happened? It is so natural, it was always there. It's not something that becomes neutral. It's not like something goes away. It's more than natural. Then you wander around thinking, 'What happened?'

Q: With this descending to the heart, is there a combustion of tendencies?

K: Not at all.

Q: You mean your tendencies are still as pre-dominant?

K: The owner who has that tendencies ceases away in the understanding of heart. Sooner or later it will be gone, so it's already gone. The first tendency is ownership of my life, my existence. The first understanding, which is the initiation of the heart, is like a broom that wipes out everything, especially that which is 'I'. If Grace wakes up, it is initiated to Itself, sooner or later Grace drops everything without any mercy – even the idea of compassion.

The main thing is the ownership burns down. It is a holocaust for the 'I' by that carelessness. It is the coolest fire you can imagine. There is not even one who cares about compassion. It doesn't care about himself or anyone else. There is relative compassion that you may experience but it still needs an owner. Compassion is that what is silence. That's why the Buddhists work on their compassion because in compassion no one can be. No one can have compassion, no one can have existence, no one can have That what one is. Compassion is erasing the idea of compassion. To be Self is to drop the idea of Self. It's an absolute drop of the idea of 'mine'. The ownership drops – that's all.

The owner, the owning, what can be owned, drops in one instant. And you are That. It is not something new. This was uninterrupted That what one is. So, it is not something that you can claim as 'my' understanding. You have nothing to claim as you already are what That is, there is no need of claiming anything. Claiming needs one who wants something and already has something and wants more. That is spirit – always greedy for more, never satisfied by what is owned. Always fearing to lose what it owns.

Fear drops when the one who owns something drops – all together. But not little by little. It's like a puff... and there is no one who realizes it. Because then there would be one too many who realize that everything is dropped. So, nothing changes.

Q: In your case it seems like the victim is gone somewhere...

K: The self-pity is gone. Self-pity is the root of everything. God knowing himself and pitying himself. Ninety-nine percent of times I laugh about the self-pity then sometimes Shiva gets angry. If you want to attract the snake that bites you, just stay in that self-pity. Then maybe it shows some mercy and kicks your ass so much that you don't know where you are anymore.

Q [Another visitor]: What do you mean God has self-pity?

K: Because from there comes a relative God who pities himself – 'poor me'. Look, God sits here crying – 'poor me'. God becomes a 'me' and then pities himself. When God knows himself as a relative person, then pitying himself to be depending. 'Poor me, I don't know myself, what can I do?' He becomes a complainer always complaining. 'Why me?' If I only could... the Almighty himself complaining that he has no power. Energy itself complaining that it has no power. Grace waiting for Grace to happen. Aww... poor Grace. [Laughter] I can make this theatrical comedy. It's like a seeker going to a master and complaining, why him why not me? It needs two to pity. So, whoever pities you, pities himself. It needs two pitiful existences to pity each other. And some call that compassion... ha, ha, ha! All of that is pity. How can I help you? Can I open my heart to you? Can I embrace you?

Q [Another visitor]: Is it a trick again to let some one be and not care?

K: It's fake again. Anyone who says, I allow you to be what-you-are, my dear! [Mocking] As if you are the queen of existence and others can do whatever you like. I give a shit about what-you-are and what-you-are-not. It happens. Sometimes one feels superior to everyone else. Shit happens. I don't care, but still there is a one I don't care about – one too many who doesn't care about someone else. It sounds good. I worked hard on my acceptance and I now accept everything. My limits are so wide that I cannot imagine that I have one. Once you realize, you laugh about the shit that you give to yourself. Cheating yourself permanently with the imaginary tricks that you play with yourself. Isn't it fun?

You always create the absolute trap for yourself and you always step into it, if you like it or not. And no one else knows yourself so very well as you know yourself. Enlightenment traps, acceptance traps, compassion traps will always be there and they seem to be so perfect and clear. Clarity – another nice trap. You think this clarity will never leave me again. Shit happens; and you cannot avoid it. Because you cannot avoid yourself, you cannot avoid the next trap you build for yourself because in that you realize yourself. Becoming the trapper, trapping, what can be trapped. And you are That! No one else can trap you so very well as you trap yourself. No one else can cheat you so very well as you cheat yourself.

Q: When one sees that this is all a block...

K: Even that becomes a trap. Whatever starts with 'if' and 'when', forget it! The only thing you cannot deny is that even by denying to exist, you have to exist, that's all! Even to say it's a block of existence, who cares? Maybe, maybe not.

Q: In the dream I saw it...

K: So, where is this bloody block now?

Q: It's here...

K: Where?

Q: No where...

K: It is a memory effect of your dream, so it's not real. Reality is never-never and Reality is uninterrupted what-it-is. It never needs to be a block of anything. It doesn't even know manifestation or no-manifestation. All of that is a memorized hear-say.

Q: It is bigger than memory...

K: What is bigger? You quantize it again. It is bigger than what? What is more or less? [Laughing] I like to make this concept and then when someone repeats it I destroy them.

Q: I am not repeating...

K: You are repeating everything that is not yours.

Q: But it was not mine either...

K: So, you are repeating something that is not yours. If it would be real, it should be here and you should present it. It's a biography of a memorized story – that's all. Even if it's not taught to you, it's like a sensational experience that you collect. It's a precious collection of your experiences. And they depend on a collector and the collector already is a phantom collector, collecting phantom experiences out of a 'me' story, having some precious experiences or not. I have no compassion with that collector, I tell you.

That's the nature of this bloody collector, hunting and collecting since the beginning of time. There is a hunter played by consciousness, collecting and hunting experiences. Making something bigger or less big, precious or less precious. My treasure! I am treasuring my bigger or not so big tra... la...la. And then I put it in my collection of precious insights. Then what is not so precious, I try to get rid of. I try to keep the happiness experiences and the ones that are not so pleasing, I try to forget.

Q: But since then, there is an acceptance...

K: But then where was this bloody acceptance before? What acceptance needs to be triggered, by what?

Q: I don't know...

K: So, it's a fleeting one; coming-going acceptance, triggered by an experience. And what kind of acceptance is that? A relative one – 'my' acceptance which was triggered by an experience.

Q: I don't say it's my experience...

K: Of course, otherwise you wouldn't talk about it. Sorry. [Laughter] No one believes me when I say sorry, not even myself. That's my destiny. [Laughing]

Everyone who sits here comes for that carelessness from those precious experiences because everyone is so loaded by those precious experiences. Everyone has been collecting that bullshit. And I tell you it's not so bad being without that personalized memory and story of whatever kind. [Laughter] Without the precious collection of gurus one has, without the precious experiences of Shakti, without the precious experiences of silence experienced with any bloody guru, it's not so bad – it's not so bad. The independent silence that never needed presence of any guru or Shakti penetrating my heart, it's not so bad. [Laughter]

It is so absolutely irrelevant; all those precious experiences, existence is a block or I am not blocked or everything is energy.

All those fleeting dream-like collection of a dream-like collector. Isn't it fantastic? And all of that would not be there anymore one day. So, it's not here-now, that's all! There is an expiry date of everything. One day it will not be there anymore and you still will be what-you-are with and without it. What you give your attention now as precious, one day it's gone anyway. And you still have to be what-you-are. So be it now, what is with and without this bloody precious treasure that you carry with you. And if you really want the treasure, be that what is the treasure itself, but not having one! [Banging on the table] [Laughter]

If I can compare the one who compares and the one that never compared anything, I would put the absolute attention to the one that never compared anything because that is what you are looking for. The rest is such a fleeting bullshit. There is such a sweetness of an absence of taste, such a tastelessness of what-you-are. And you cannot imagine what-you-are and what-you-are-not. So, you don't need this imagination to be what-you-are. How can you believe in the bullshit that you tell yourself? But you can; that's the problem. How can you not believe yourself? You become a believer in yourself and by believing, you left yourself.

By believing, you became a leaf on the tree of existence, but you are not even the tree. Then you expect fruits from that bloody tree. It is a dry, empty bloody tree that will never bring any fruits to you. It will never satisfy you, this tree-nity (trinity), this trio *infernale* starting with awareness, then becomes consciousness and then becomes the world. You become your own devil by believing in this trio *infernale* of your so-called realization, that it can make you more or less than you already are.

Q [Another visitor]: Why do they say that a desire fulfilled breeds more desires?

K: It's like karma yoga, trying to un-knot the knots of your desires. By opening one knot, you create ten others.

Q: Shouldn't it be the opposite?

K: That's what you think. The instant you think you can do

something and you succeed in doing that, you make the first one who thinks he has to un-knot something stronger. The un-knotter which is itself a knot becomes stronger by succeeding in un-knotting the knots. By your even succeeding in un-knotting the desires, the first desirer becomes stronger. Then for sure, he wants to get rid of all the desires. But he cannot get rid of himself. That is the primal, the first desire – the desirer, the owner. Even when the owner drops everything, he cannot drop himself. Even by succeeding in dropping, by becoming more tolerant, he becomes superior. 'I am detached now'. Then he is totally attached to being detached and this attachment gets stronger and stronger.

You believe that you can do something and you even succeed in it. That is meant by that the first desirer becomes stronger.

Q: So, by fulfilling the desires, the desirer becomes stronger?

K: By not fulfilling them too. The fulfilment of desires means you succeed in something and then the successor tries to suck more. The succeeder is the sucker, succeeding in sucking, tries to suck more. It's like you suck the universal tit of the universe and there is a moment of fulfilment and you want to have it again and again. So, your desire becomes stronger for fulfilment. That is the oneness experience. The desire gets stronger by the fulfilment of oneness. Then you always compare everything to that. Then everything becomes like – 'poor me'. Then it was so nice and now look at poor 'me'.

Q: But does the opposite work?

K: You may try. Let's see. That's the way of resignation. You resign, resign, resign. But who resigns the resigner? And who needs to resign the resigner? The awareness 'I' signs-in to that tendency of gaining something and one day he concludes that less is more. Then the resigner resigns. Then he stays in that samadhi of awareness and one day he signs-in again, interest happens again. Then he goes back to trying to know himself. This is the spider Ramana talks about. The spider withdrawing everything and then out of the blue starts to spin again. Trying to catch itself in the net which is spun by itself. In one instant the spider sees that it cannot be caught by his own web, withdraws it. Then not knowing what happened before, it starts to spin again. No way out! You are still in that imaginary happy end. [Laughter]

And I tell you that very imaginary happy end is hell and you cannot get out of it because you became a devil to yourself. You created your own hell. God believing in himself – hell-elujah. He becomes his own teacher, his own guru, his own master. Enslaving himself with the idea that he can ever know himself, that something has to happen, that desires have to go to be what he is. Unlimited slavery! God enslaved by his own ideas.

Do you really think God has a beginning of what is existence? It's all fiction. Having or having not – who cares? This is a relationship. The moment you have an end, you have a relationship with yourself, you are married to yourself. Then for sure you want to have a happy end of this relationship. That's love. Loving caring about yourself and wanting to have a happy ending – happy, happy ever after. Me, myself and I, agreeing to oneself. In an absolute agreement to myself, I am absolutely happy and never be unhappy ever after that.

Q: That's generally all the stories end...

K: Not all the stories.

Q: Almost...

K: But not all.

Q: So, is it a conditioning to look for a happy ending?

K: Whatever looks for a happy ending imagines that he has a beginning. And whatever imagines that he has a beginning for sure, by the loving caring business tries to make a happy end out of it. The instant you are something that has a beginning, like this body has a beginning, the soul has a beginning, even imagining that you exist, you doubt that existence. Then you look for the beginning because you want to control yourself. No way out! Then you are very busy. In this loving-caring business for yourself, you want to have the best for yourself. The best guru, the best understanding, the best inner-vision, the best outer-vision. Only the best is good enough for what-you-are. Not less, only the best. That is called love. What else?

But the best cannot be found – thank God. So, you will never be satisfied by the second-best. The second-best is the awareness. It's not bad but it's only second-best and there is no satisfaction in second-best. The satisfaction is only in that goodness itself, second-best is not good enough. Only goodness itself is good enough for you to be and any other experience of clarity is all second-best, if at all, and never good enough.

The instant you see it would never be good enough, suddenly you are the goodness itself which is only that what is good enough for you. There is a satisfaction which is never depending on the so-called understanding of any kind of sensational block of existence – manifest or un-manifest and all of what you can imagine. In that instance you fuck it all. It is really like – so what?

So, you win the enlightenment lottery before you are what-you-are. When you are what-you-are, no one cares about the bloody enlightenment anymore, of any kind of deepest or final understanding tra...la...la... There will never be any final tra...la...la... What to do?

Q: It is ridiculous to see that someone cares about understanding, about enlightenment. It just looks like a game...

K: You think there is a game?

Q: It appears to be but ultimately there is none...

K: Enjoy the stupidity, that's all I ask. What do you think I am doing here? I am enjoying the ignorance which is permanently coming out of what I am and cannot make me more or less as I am. Whatever you can pronounce is ignorance. So, who cares? What a freedom of ignorance, that none of what you experience can touch what-you-are or do anything to what-you-are. You are always in spite of the ignorance and the ignorance is like... shit happens! So what?

You are absolute stupid as your nature is absolute stupid. But who cares to be stupid or not? If by all that stupidity you cannot know yourself or not know yourself – Hallelujah! There is a presence and absence of stupidity, but who cares? That is out-rooting the idea that one day there will be an end of ignorance. If you see that there will never be any end of ignorance, it ends because you end in it. Because the interest drops absolutely in that ignorance – that's all. By that interest you have the expectation that one day the ignorance will stop and you will be the knowledge; which is then a new knowledge.

The ignorance is never ending and I mean it. Whatever I can find and whatever I found is ignorance and I am unlimited in my ignorance and there is no beginning and no end of ignorance. There is an absolute rest in that ignorance. I am absolutely happy that I cannot know myself. There will always be ignorance about my self and that is joy. As I cannot know myself, no one else can know myself. And as I cannot control myself, no one else will control myself. That is called moksha. Nothing else can satisfy That what-you-are as that. So, be happy that you cannot know yourself and so will no one else – never-ever.

So I am talking about [Blowing in the wind]... Maybe I can just give the taste of the joy of irrelevance of speaking and you may join in the irrelevance of listening. Irrelevance of question and irrelevance of answering. Enjoying absolutely about all the happenings and non-happenings of whatever kind and any kind of special and non-special experience may drop: if it has to happen and the next sip of coffee is the next realization of what-you-are and nothing is more or less in that.

There is only a quality of absolute existence being the absolute experiencer experiencing himself in every possible way and there will never be any ending to that. No way out!

Q: What a relief!

K: You don't have to polish the pearl of your bloody understanding. As if now I gave you the pearl and you have to care about it. In the presence of a heart master your heart opens and then you have to care about your open heart because it is bleeding all the time. [Laughter]

I like all the stories. Thank God no one needs them because one day they will be gone as nothing, even the story of Christ being crucified. One day there will be no one who would remember Buddha or Christ or anyone and still existence will be what-it-is and they all said that. I am not the first one who says that. I just repeat myself infinite times, and nothing happens.

Everyone waits for a breakthrough, that one day I will be so loaded with experiences that I would break through, the holywood-way. [Laughing]

Q: Ramana says do everything with indifference. Dispassion is your nature...

K: You can say That what is the existence without the second cannot have passion because it needs two to have passion – a lover and a beloved. In the nature of the love, nature of loving and the nature of beloved there is no passion and without passion, there is no suffering. But any presence of a lover who starts to love himself becomes a caretaker about himself – loving-caring about what-one-is. I am what? That is the question you imagine as the highest you can have in love – knowing yourself. And by that, you are active.

There is a passionate love in it. By that passion you love yourself and by that one day you hate that you love yourself. Both come together in that passion. Loving and hating is one and the same because loving makes you depending and you hate to love yourself. That you are glued to the idea that one day you would know yourself. One day you regret that you even started to know yourself. Then you want to kill yourself. Meditation is trying to kill that lover inside because you think that I would be better-off without the idea of me. I will be happy without 'me'. That's called meditation. Then you may even reach – I am nothingness and nothingness doesn't care. Trap by trap by trap. You are like a tap dancer – trap, trap, trap.

Q: So, there is no meditation?

K: I tell you, you cannot not meditate. Meditation is 24 by 7 by 365 and not sometime sitting down and closing your eyes. Meditation is your bloody nature when you are awake.

Q: But until we get to that stage...

K: What stage? Who goes to that stage? There is no one who does that. There is no meditator.

Q: That's too high for me...

K: There is a survival system running and then you say it's not for me, it's too high for me, I better look another way.

Q: Let's take baby steps...

K: You are not here in a kindergarten and you are not here to be pampered I tell you. Everyone looks for someone who pampers him. Everyone is looking for a God or the highest guru or the highest self to be pampered by it, embraced by it and then being pampered for ever – existence takes care. Ha...ha...ha... As if existence cares about how you are! [Laughing] My goodness!

Existence could not care less about your so-called mood. Do you really think existence takes care about anything?

Q: Whose existence?

K: Who is taking care about whom?

Q: It seems like the entire dream has already been dreamt...

K: Who says so? Maybe not.

Q: But these *deja vu* experiences...

K: Even that you can say are imaginary experiences. There is an imaginary *deja vu* and an imaginary no *deja vu*.

Q: But I want to land somewhere...

K: I know. [Laughter]

Q: You are preventing my plan from landing...

K: That's why you become a complainer because now you drive the com-plane. [Laughter] Then you think that by complaining you will land somewhere.

Q: At least for refuelling... [Laughter]

K: This is like a petrol station with a sign – Closed forever. [Laughter] No refill.

Q: And crash somewhere...

K: You are the crash test dummy. One day you will crash, don't worry. Who cares when?

Q: Can I say 'me'? [Laughter]

K: You are like a running model and one day it will run out and existence will still be what existence is without any idea of complaining or not-complaining, of landing or not landing somewhere. It's a running out model.

Q: Yeah. In fifty years it wouldn't make difference at all...

K: As I say, you are already a running around tombstone. You should have a tattoo: RIP. [Laughter] A tombstone who thinks he is alive. A walking corpse. Whatever you see there will be an end to that. Whatever you experience, there will be an end to it. Whatever was there or not there, one day you will be without it. So, be without it, right now, here-now. And who cares if it's there or not if you are absolutely independent of all that landing and complaining bastard you think you are?

Q [Another visitor]: In one way I think consciousness totally cares about you...

K: No. It is totally blind. It doesn't even know you.

Q: It cares because I Am That...

K: Who is that?

Q: Consciousness...

K: What consciousness? Who wants to be the bloody consciousness which is already ignorance. Who wants to be an imaginary consciousness? Then saying I am that imaginary consciousness. You have to imagine it otherwise it wouldn't be there. Who cares about the imaginary consciousness which says I Am That? There was never any care-taker in existence. Existence never cares about existence. What an idea! The care-taker taking care of whatever can be taken care about is a dream. And who cares about a dream care-taker which is a good care-taker or bad care-taker taking care about what?

Q: The point was not to make a separation...

K: But you separate already. If you say existence would care, you would separate existence because for caring it needs two.

Q: In that way it is not possible to speak anything...

K: But I am speaking with you. [Laughter] That's why I say be quiet and don't see.

Q [Another visitor]: I don't know about your existence but my existence takes care of me...

K: I tell you I am not jealous about that bloody existence at all. [Laughter] The relative existence that takes care about another relative existence, what can it be? A care-taker of what?

Q: So, I am alone. Even my existence doesn't care... [Laughter]

K: You may say that you are absolutely isolated. There is no second and no one can bear that. There can be no idea in that carelessness. But you may say that is the way out of the absolute self-pity.

By destroying whatever is not needed, that is called compassion, by not letting any special dream-like thing to remain. When Grace wakes up, watch out, because Grace shows no pity. And Grace doesn't even know grace. That Grace-lessness drops and kicks everything.

Q: When Grace wakes up...

K: It wakes up when it wakes up, in spite of what happened before. It is never because of your so-called understanding or action or inner intuition. Whatever you can do, when Grace wakes up, it drops you as nothing. Never needed, never wanted. You disappear like a dew drop in a hot sun. It evaporates... and what happens? Nothing.

There is a nice story that one day the night goes to God and complains that when sun rises, it chases me away. It's like ignorance as night has to go when the sun rises. Then God goes to the sun and asks why are you so naughty? Why do you always destroy the night? And sun asks – What night? When there is sun, there will never be any night or shadow of any kind of ignorance. The sun doesn't even know that it has something to destroy. They call it the rising of the inner sun which is existence itself. It burns out everything, just by its nature, by destroying all the darkness in an instant. As if there was never anything there. There was never any knowledge of ignorance in that. Where there is the sun of the Self, there never was and never will be any ignorance. And it wakes up when it wakes up. That's why it's called as rising of the inner sun which you cannot attract.

If this inner sun rises, it burns out whatever can be burnt out, but not by knowing anything. It doesn't care about it. It doesn't even know that something burns out in its presence or the presense. Then you hope that you can survive in that. Ha...ha...ha... Your precious experiences of the block-like something would be evaporated in a split second. My precious story of whatever... once upon a time, I had this experience... blah...blah...blah – Puff. As if nothing ever happened. There was nothing. And the rest is what? Fishing in the dark. Blind masters leading blind disciples, blinded by... what?

That split-second is splitting the second absolutely by not splitting anything, but simply being what-it-is.

Q: So there is no rising of the sun? Because now you talk about an imagination of maybe something that would happen in future...

K: Yeah. But that they call as rising of the inner sun which cannot be attracted or prevented. It's like the Self wakes up to itself by being what-it-is, burning out whatever is ignorance. In that every idea of what-you-are and what-you-are-not gets evaporated in one instant. There is no process in it.

Q [Another visitor]: It rises on its own?

K: Simply by being what-it-is.

Q: And in the mean while?

K: Enjoy yourself as you cannot do anything anyway.

Q [Another visitor]: But this is something in time. Show it to me now...

K: That I don't have to show because that I Am anyway.

Q: So Am I. You put that in time again, rising of the sun in future...

K: Yes I do and it doesn't matter.

Q: But now I believe it...

K: You don't have to believe it. If you know me, I create a concept and next moment I destroy it. And if you listen to me whatever I say or pronounce is unlimited ignorance anyway. So who cares?

Q: But then we still wait for something to happen in future...

K: Then you believe in what I said and you still wait for the sun to rise.

Q: No thanks... [Laughter]

K: Now you don't believe in anything. [Laughter] It sounded like you reached a final point... don't believe in anything. No. The beauty of what-it-is is that it can talk so much bullshit and still it doesn't matter. Calling something a rising sun or anything, it makes no difference. It really doesn't matter. I can pronounce the biggest poetry of the rising sun and in the next moment – puff – as nothing.

In a way it is the simple pointer that it is in spite of your bloody understanding or not-understanding. Already that is the rising sun, if there is this understanding that you are in spite of it. This already is a rising sun, of initiation of that what is the Heart. And by that initiation, it burns out everything. With this initiation, if the concepts are dry enough, they fly away. Normally they are wet with the permanent self-pity. Then it doesn't burn so well. That's all. [Laughing]

If God is in its self-pity then the concepts are still wet. But if the self-pity is gone and there is a resignation – Who cares? Maybe then there is a little – puff. Any word can trigger that, you never know what. That's why maybe I talk so much. It's like an infinite talking and you never know what is the trigger of that. It's not like putting up a sentence together, like wisdom. You never know. Maybe even the most bullshit joke can sometimes trigger that.

It's like a wood-pecker pecking... knock, knock, knock... anybody home? And suddenly there is a total insight that nobody is at home. You can knock as much as you like and no one will answer. [Laughter]

Q [Another visitor]: I am looking at my patterns in life that create different situations. Is there any relevance in it? Do you have to clear them?

K: Esoterically yes, if you want to become a better person there are many ways of getting rid of the blocks. But I am not the right person for that. If you are hungry you eat something what you like so that your body is not troubled. So there are relative advantages in all that. And everyone is looking for that. It is called the loving-caring of the auto mobile that you are driving.

Q: Is that a problem?

K: You may take care of your automobile. There is nothing wrong with that. But it is not in your hand if you maintain it right or wrong. One day it will be gone anyway. But until then, you enjoy it, you drive it, you experience it, different points of view coming out of the relative 'I' position. Then you change it to another position and you look from there. The Absolute seer doesn't look from one position alone; it's like an infinite eye of God: the ownership idea that this body idea will be gone one day and you still will be what-you-are. Nothing wrong or right in it.

It is simply realizing the infinite possibilities that it will simply be different. But by all the differences and changes, you still are what-you-are. The Existence which is your nature is not changed by all the differences. Existence will never rise because more existence is not possible here-now. Existence is already that what-it-is, it never has to rise. But the relative consciousness, there is like a rising sun in a relative frame of time. And by that rising sun, consciousness may even realize that it can never realize as it is ever realized. But even that comes and goes. Even the realization of rising of the inner sun is a relative one.

Q: So, what about the preferences in the relative realm?

K: Just enjoy the preferences. If you ask me, just see that they don't belong to you. They are temporary belongings. But your naked existence is here-now what-it-is and one day you would be naked again because all the belongings and all the dressings and all your precious items will be gone one day and you still will be what-you-are.

Q: Isn't this a collection of ideas?

K: It is a collection of experiences. You dress yourself with experiences. You want the better ones and you want to get rid of the worn out ones. Your inner child needs attention. Then you behave or dress yourself so that you can get this love.

Q: Is it possible to improve that process?

K: Yes. But it would be an improved phantom. Why not? Let the phantom be improved or disproved. Be generous... as your nature is generosity itself. Let the phantom improve. Drive a better car or drive a motor-bike. Even not allowing yourself... allow yourself that.

I tell you, without the absolute acceptance of That what-it-is, you could not have one idea about any preferences or any experience of preferences, there would be no owner, there would be no treasuring. Acceptance is all there is and without the acceptance of the Existence, you could not even lift your little finger. In that way, there is no 'me' doing anything. Without the totality of existence playing all that could be played out, you cannot even lift your eyebrow or having a preference. Even the owner, owning, what can be owned, can only be there with the acceptance of that. Reality realizing itself as that. So what? And nothing has to change for that. And even you trying to improve is fine because even that idea of improving comes out of the same origin as everything. And who doubts that? And who thinks it is... whatever?

The origin of whatever is, is that Absolute Existence and without that, nothing ever is.

Q: Within that there is an experience of choice?

K: There is an experience of choice, but no one who has it. There is an experience of no-choice but no one who has it. There is no ownership in all that. That's freedom – the absence of ownership. There is no second edition of existence. Existence is what-you-are and existence is realizing itself in whatever possible and impossible ways. I can only repeat that. And there is no second edition – that's all.

And as you exist, and you know that by heart that you exist, no one has to tell you that, That never needs any understanding or no-understanding, any rising or no-rising, Nothing has to be changed for the existence to be what existence is. And by heart you know that you exist. That knowledge is undisturbable and cannot be created or destroyed. So, it is absolutely independent of so-called experience at all. So, rest in that where no one can rest.

What will be done, will be done. But by that doing, nothing is done by anyone. But still, there will be an experience of an experiencer, experiencing whatever can be experienced. But already the experiencer is already experienced by what-you-are. And that can never be changed by any difference of experiencing. So, enjoy yourself, because this never had any beginning and never would have any end.

Joy is your nature and in joy, joy appears. Joy is all there is! More joy cannot bring you more joy and less joy cannot bring you less. But there is an imaginary experience of more joy and less joy. But by more joy, you don't become more joy and by less joy you don't become less joy. Existence experiences itself as more existence or less existence, but by experience of more existence it doesn't become more, and by experience of less existence, not less. So, the quality of what-you-are has nothing to gain. There is an experience of more and less, that's all. But by experience of more, or less, there is nothing to gain or to lose. But there is no choice in it.

The choicelessness creates a chooser choosing what is chosen. But whatever the chooser chooses what is chosen, choicelessness cannot be reached. But choicelessness is always a goal for whatever you try to do. Whatever you wish for is a wish for wishlessness because that is ananda or happiness – the absence of one who needs or doesn't need anything, of the one who is happy or not happy. That is happiness itself.

But out of that what is happiness itself, the happy or the unhappy one arises. So, it is rising and disappearing all the time, the happy and the unhappy one; sometimes happy sometimes unhappy. But already the unhappy one comes out of that what is happiness. So, even the unhappiness is the happiness because the nature of existence is happiness. So, what can happen in all those happenings? Only happiness experiencing happiness, even in unhappiness. So, even the unhappy or the happy one in its nature is happiness.

I can only talk to death to what can be talked to death. That what is Life itself can never be talked to death. It never needs to remember anything. But that is worst for the ego that no one cares what the ego does. The sinner is only alive because there is someone caring about him and I tell you existence never cared about anyone. In existence there is no care taking system running. The care taker, the care taking, what can be taken care about, is dream-like experiences. But no one cares about how the experiences develop or how anyone gets enlightened.

Q [Another visitor]: What is a montage point?

K: When you were born there was a random seer which was not fixed to any personality. Then your mother always tries to hit on one point, you are my son, you are born in this family, whatever. That conditioning hits on one point and then suddenly the personality is more and more stabilized on that point because the circumstance always confirms you and makes it bigger, like a canyon. Then you are trapped in that canyon.

Then all shamanism is trying is trying to make that undone. So that the personal story becomes a flat line again so that perception moves freely in whatever is that. That is a montage point which is a conditioning of consciousness which is like hitting on one point, like you are the son of a mother having a personal story. Then they try to undo the personal story by breathing techniques. Even the tantra is the same; getting rid of the personal story of whatever you can imagine. Then it feels like a flat line again and then it is a free floating perception which has no personal story anymore. Even the drugs take you out of that montage point and make you free and then by whatever, you get back. And if it doesn't come back, you end up in a mad house.

So, the healthy person knows where he belongs. The healthy person is very established in this montage point and a mad person is more free floating, not knowing where he belongs. Now the psychotherapists want to bring you back to the healthy spot. So that you know who you are and you are safe there, that existence cares about you. So if the freedom of the Heart suddenly happens and the montage point rises, then you end up in a mad-house. No personal point of view anymore, there is pointlessness, there is no past, no future. Then comes the psychotherapist that tells you who you are. Then it gets deeper and deeper and established in one spot. A crazy one telling another crazy one that you belong there. I am crazy and you are crazy. It's like a membership of craziness. You have to remember who you are so that you can be a member of the mad house of existence.

Any moment you are born, you are in the craziness in the mad house of the universe; being crazy after yourself.

Q: Can the therapist be a pimp for Reality?

K: Maybe. Whoever sits in front of a picture and saying this is my lineage is a prostitute selling himself for his pimps. In Germany we say, whoever walks the line is a prostitute. It's like the prostitute walking up and down waiting for a big spender.

17th June 2007, Talk 2
Ladakh, India

As Long As A Teacher Has Something To Teach, He Has Something To Learn

Q: Sometimes there is an experience of a sense of humour…

K: And sometimes not.

Q: Everything is happening on its own and there is no one doing it…

K: It's like yes and no. Doing it or not, both are not right. Who says that no one is doing it? You can say there is a relative 'I' who is doing it. But for the Absolute, whatever is done is done by simply waking up.

Q: From the relative perspective of 'me', no one is doing it…

K: Who needs to understand that no one is doing it?

Q: It seems promising…

K: There is a promise of peace but even that is bad. The promise of peace which is an understanding confirms that there is one who can understand and in that understanding needs peace.

Q; There is a sense of humour in this…

K: That you can call it a divine comedy. It is simply like to understand the joke. But you are the joker who understands that you are the joker, joking, and out of that joker all the jokes come. That is the absolute sense of humour.

Q: So, what is this absolute sense of humour?

K: That you can call as an absolute sense of humour of Shiva, having the fun of building everything and then destroying it, without caring about it.

Q: Is that another part of experience?

K: No. This is uninterrupted. The sense of humour of Existence is never-never. This is Silence, which is happiness, being that what is humour which has no humour. Even in the suffering experience in the background there is always the enjoyer. 'Look at him, he suffers really deep today'. You better be that which enjoys the silence without any interruption and nothing happens in that silence.

Q: It is funny sometimes…

K: It's not sometimes funny, it is fun itself.

Q: You must be laughing inside the world quite a bit…

K: I don't have to show it, sometimes I cannot hide it. But it is the same with you. You sit here so that I trigger what is hiding in the back.

Q: Sure, I want to laugh…

K: Yes. But by wanting to laugh, you cannot laugh.

Q: Then we get into a problem…

K: Then we are talking about the nature of fun; the nature of absolute laughter is helplessness. It cannot want what it wants because it doesn't even know how to want.

Q: There is an openness and expansiveness, the more you experience it, the more the sense of humour comes…

K: Even with that you make a little hope inside that something comes and something has to happen. You think there would be a better circumstance and you would be established in something what is always enjoying itself.

Whatever you say, there has to be the Seer – the absolute perception – without which there would be no talker, no talking, no listener, nothing can happen without that absolute perception. That is uninterrupted, with and without perceiving. The relative perceiver which perceives is already sometimes there and sometimes not, but perception is even when it is not perceiving anything, because the absolute Seer does not need to enjoy anything to be what-it-is or what-he-is. It doesn't matter if you call it 'he' or 'it', you can call it personal or impersonal. That is never-never and the rest is sometimes like this and sometimes like that, always changing.

This is the joy of Silence, which is uninterrupted. It can never be interrupted by dream-like drama of a sufferer suffering about something or enjoying something or not. This never needs to enjoy itself. There is a joy without an interruption which is your nature and it cannot be disturbed. It is not like someone enjoying the movie or drama and becomes sarcastic. No. It is simply there as joy, in spite of how it is That, never because. So, it is not as if it has to enjoy the scenery. It is like a screen, never-never. Never needs any projection of sense of humour or any idea to be what-it-is.

Q: Why should it have the characteristic of joy?

K: The definition of joy is the absence of one who has to enjoy himself or not. It is the joy of Silence. The happiness itself which is the absence of any necessity of enjoying oneself. Happiness is another word for moksha, that what is knowledge which never needs anyone to be what one is. That is knowledge, joy, happiness, the Self, whatever you call it. It never has to exist to exist. There is no need, no necessity of any kind. That is Silence and Silence is never-never. There is no second to it and it cannot be disturbed by itself. That is peace, joy, knowledge, and that is your nature.

Any moment you imagine to have the need to have joy, you become a relative enjoyer. In that instant you commit suicide. You step out of your absolute nature a relative one. But can you avoid that?

Q: Seemingly no...

K: So, shit happens. Then I sit here and ask, did something happen for you by imaginary going out and being an imaginary sufferer having an imaginary suffering about something? Did your nature change? Absolutely not, so nothing happens! That's why Buddha calls it a divine accident and in the accident you cannot avoid the accident of waking up. But your nature is not changed by that, that's all. Your nature is still the unborn, absolute never changing existence which is not aware of what-it-is. In the first awareness, nothing happens. In the first idea of awareness, the idea of sufferer, you cannot not go out.

Q: Then there are so many ideas as if something did happen...

K: Because there is a root thought of 'I' which grows like hell and creates all the belief systems. All the trees start with the root thought 'I', the trinity of thoughts. Then there is a thought that you can go back by going back to the root. That is the nature of that belief system, of that tree. The tree grows leafs, there are be-leaf (belief) system of concepts simply because there is a tree and there is a root thought 'I' and the tree starts from there.

Q: In fact I feed the tree in a way...

K: Then you are asked to go back to the beginning and in the beginning does something happen for what-you-are? Does your nature become relative by the experience of becoming relative?

Q: It is a difficult question...

K: No, it's not difficult. It is absolutely natural that you may experience that even by the experience of separation, you are not separate. Prior to the experience of relative 'I', there has to be that Experiencer 'you are', and you cannot not be that. So, even prior to the experience of relative 'I' thought, you have to be there as you are. Then comes the experience of 'I' and out of that comes 'I Am' and then whatever follows. So, in the beginning nothing happens. Your nature already has to be there so even the beginning can be.

And after the beginning, you are still what-you-are. That is called Silence, which is never-never which is your very nature and that you cannot not be. So be what you are.

That's what Ramana meant when he says, 'Be what you are', then you of course ask, 'How can I be what I am?' What a stupid question! But how can you not? The dance is still on. These can only be pointers and this can never make you what-you-are. Even understanding, it comes and goes.

Q [Another visitor]: When you have an experience of suffering in the body that takes precedence over what-you-are, there seems to be a part of personality that tries to go back to what-you-are and tries to use it as a rescue...

K: Out of the missing comes longing and out of longing comes a seeker.

Q: So it is always the seeker that's trying to get home...

K: No. It is the Self that falls in love again with itself. You fall in love with a relative idea and only love can make you so stupid to make you leave what-you-are, and you cannot not fall in love.

Q: So, the circumstance takes you out of your nature?

K: No. It's not circumstance, it is love. Nature of existence is love and out of the love comes the lover. And what can the lover do? The lover has to fall in love, loving caring about the beloved. Out of love comes the lover, loving and the beloved. But if you end up here, the love has turned bitter because it seems like you lost what-you-are. It seems that you are separated as a lover taking yourself as separate from your beloved. That is the trap. That is the divine hypnosis that there is a lover separate from the beloved. And it is so strong and so real because you take yourself as a lover separate from the beloved.

In Gnosticism it is like the snake looking at its own moving tail and thinking that it is the second snake. From then on there is a loving and hating. From there on, you love the world or you hate the world. But there is a loving-caring 'I', that's its nature. Then you are trapped in the trap that you are separated because you think as a lover you are different from your beloved; subject-object. Then you are in trouble. Then you miss your absolute nature and by missing the absolute nature you want to be again what is never missing anything. You cannot avoid the trap.

Q: And then what?

K: Then one day you bite in your own tail – self-abite-ance – then you realize that the lover is not different from the beloved and both disappear in to that what is the lover and the beloved. This is the Self-realization of Consciousness, which is the lover, loving and the beloved. There is no one loving after that, both disappear in that by being That. But there is no oneness. Oneness needs two. But if the lover and the beloved are not different, then That is. That is Self-realization, when you are the lover not different from the beloved, because the essence of the lover and the essence of the beloved both disappear. This is the total annihilation of the idea of separation, of ego. Because ego is separation or mind. Never was there any mind because mind is separation and there was never any separation. This is not something new; this is what-you-are. But in separation, you miss That. But as much as you want oneness, even oneness confirms separation.

Even when you totally accept the beloved, it is still separation. As long as there is one expecting something else, it is separation. Acceptance is your nature but acceptance doesn't know any acceptance and it doesn't have to accept anything. But if there is someone who believes that he has to understand something and accept something, there is already separation. Even a jñani who understands everything, is one too many.

Q: But there is also a fear to give that up...

K: Yes because you fear that you give up love or you lose your existence because you think you cannot exist without a second. What a trap!

Q: So, what to do about this fear?

K: What a stupid idea. Whatever you do against it, you confirm that there is one who needs something to do.

Q: So, nothing to do?

K: Nothing is too much and everything is too less. Even nothing to do is still a concept. That has never done anything. Doing or not doing is confirming the doer. Loving or not loving confirms the lover and the lover is always one lover too many.

Q: So, there really is a trap...

K: It is a divine trap. It is so perfect since it comes out of perfection and the trap is as perfect as you are. And it is not meant that you realize yourself. [Laughter] It is not in the plan. It is not in the dream. It is like a divine accident. It is like a loop hole out of the law of action-reaction of love, you as a lover drop out of that love. It was not meant like this. But you try your best to do the impossible.

Q: So, you can't become accident-prone?

K: The accident already happened, you cannot avoid it. That's the point, the accident already happened. You woke up. You started to realize yourself as a lover, loving yourself. Now you think you can avoid the accident? It's too late! Accident happened. You already hit the trinity of existence but now you want to undo it. That makes you a seeker. That is the death wish – 'Now I want to be prior to the accident so that I can avoid the accident'. By trying to avoid the accident that really makes you suffer about the accident. Just see that the accident happened, so what? Shit happens!

But does that matter? Does your nature become more or less or anything? Does it change anything of that Existence you are? Does it matter if there is that love affair or not? This is your Absolute love affair. You started this love affair with yourself and maybe even that is an idea. Maybe it never started and will never end. You manifest yourself, realize yourself in this love affair as a creator, creating, what can be created. This trinity is what-you-are. You are

That and you cannot escape That. So what to do? Or not to do?

That's why I say enjoy yourself because it may take a while. Maybe it never started and will never end, your love affair – me, myself and 'I' – having or not having a good time. Who cares?

Q: The 'me' comes after the thought...

K: That is an old story.

Q: But it helps me...

K: Who needs to be helped?

Q: ME!

K: This is the working and thinking... tra...la...la... Am I the doer or the non-doer? I am not in this doing or non-doing business. I really don't care. I am not here for any personal therapy at all. It just permanently confirms the one who needs to be helped. The ghost always needs a confirmation that the ghost needs help.

Q: But I see that the ghost comes after...

K: After what?

Q: After whatever happens...

K: What? Did something happen? First you confirm the happening and then after that you say you are not the doer. Both are confirmation of happening. Then comes one who is stupid enough to takes it as his action.

Q: But being in the world it helps a lot...

K: Who is in the world? Show me one.

Q: I cannot...

K: You see, it is all fiction! But you try to understand the fiction in order to make the fiction a better world or a better 'me', a more comfortable 'me'. You always try to make a better comfortable and harmonic life. You even take understanding as a tool of controlling your harmony. Of course that is the nature of the little 'me', trying to get comfort.

Q: But yet it seems like it loses its power with understanding...

K: No. It gets stronger by believing that he understood something.

Q: It is not a matter of understanding but a matter of realizing...

K: But who has to realize something and then having a better life? Always comparing before and after, before I was stupid and now I am less stupid. But it is not about knowledge, it is always about getting less stupid, that's all. But who cares about being less stupid. You are stupid enough to believe in the process of getting from some place to some other place. Then you say it helps you. No I cannot allow that over here. I know it's tricky.

Q: Now you try to make me angry...

K: I like to make the beast angry because when the beast shows up, the devil shows up and you see what is really behind it. It's always a devil, the beast who wants to control; even by being nice. You know that I try to get this beast out all the time. This beast can hide behind the understanding so very well and making a nice mask of compassion... ha... ha... ha...

And I know the beast so very well because I am the beast itself.

Q: Full of compassion...

K: [Laughing] Let the passion come, that is compassion. And passion is suffering. Such a big trickster! Cannot get any better. Understanding becomes another golden cow. You pray to some understanding, you pray to knowledge, you pray to wisdom, you pray to whatever and you make it your God. The intellect then becomes another God. You try to be saved by slavery. By the slavery of thinking that I can get more comfort, you make harmony as your God, you make freedom as your God, understanding, truth, all you can imagine, you make it your God and the instant you make it your God, you are enslaved by that. Even the sense of humour you make it your God.

It is strange how many Gods one can create! How many icons one creates, having a better personal life, having a better God becomes the world. All the idealistic ideas of how the existence has to be and what needs to happen.

Q [Another visitor]: Somehow I try to fill the void with these Gods...

K: Who has to avoid the void? Only the bloody devil, because in the void the devil cannot be. God comes out of the idea of devil. The devil creates God so that the devil can survive. It is all a survival strategy for the first ghost you think you are and the ghost always needs a God and suffering is the best. Even the end of suffering becomes a God; the end of whatever... The end of old days.

And you cannot get rid of this guy, that's the worst. As much as you want to get rid of that phantom, it is there.

Q: Even when you don't want to get rid of it, it doesn't go away...

K: Yeah. But who needs the phantom to go away, that's the question? What kind of existence would it be that needs the phantom to disappear to exist? That's the absolute 'who cares'?

Q: You can't do anything about it...

K: If at all, then only That what is the absolute existence could do something, but it has no interest. So, it could do something but it has no interest because there is no need. For that what is existence there is no necessity of anything to come or to go. And that what has a necessity already is part of this bloody... So what?

So, this is a no-win situation. That what never has to win anything has no interest and that what needs to win something cannot, because it has no power. That what is power has no interest and that has no power wants something. Ha... ha... ha...

Q: So everything is hopeless...

K: It is hopelessness.

Q [Another visitor]: Every time I try to understand something I feel like shit and then I forget it and then feel okay...

K: That's what you should do; forget your bloody understanding – if you can. But you cannot.

Q: Because it comes and goes...

K: It is like a boomerang, it hits you again. As much as you want to throw it away, it comes back. As much as you want to throw that 'I' and you think now it's gone forever, you turn around and think 'Now I am free, everything is so clear now'. Then it boomerangs and hits you back. There is an absolute ease and the moment you step out of it, there is the disease again. Then you experience the helplessness that you can neither stay in the ease or the disease, it's always switching.

Q: Yesterday I saw this endless switching between ease and disease and thought this is it...

K: You think this is it and the next moment, 'Oh no shit again!'. The main thing is in both you have to exist; existence is unchanged by all that swinging. This is the swinger club of existence and you are the only member. Shit! [Laughter]

Q [Another visitor]: You swing with yourself...

K: But you are looking for a partner to swing with you. Then you imagine one and then you forget that you had only imagined that one. Shiva creates the puppet house to play with puppets. Then he plays so intensively that he forgets and himself becomes a puppet. Then suddenly he is a puppet under puppets. Then he tries to get out of the puppet house. But Shiva was never in the puppet house, he created the puppet house. Then the cosmic energy played with the puppet house, but by playing it, it forgets that which is the origin of the puppet house. Then he says suddenly – Who am I? What am I doing here? Now I have to find a way out of this bloody puppet house. Then he imagines that there must be a God since there is a puppet house. There must be a creator of this puppet house. Maybe he takes me out if I behave like a good puppet.

The Origin of everything imagining and becoming a puppet and imagining that I have to get out again. What a joke! The Absolute energy itself imagining that it needs someone to take him out of what is created by him. How stupid can one get? I can only point – come on, you imagined to be a puppet. You never went out by the imaginary going out of this puppet house. It is all created by you! You are the origin of the puppet house and the God that comes out of that imagination. Now you complain how the puppet house is. [Laughter] As everyone complains, you become one of the complainers and become one of the six billion who want to make this world a paradise as they want it to be. Then you run around the world looking for a better puppet house.

Shiva hoping to get out of the puppet house, what an idea! The lover thinking, 'When I control the beloved, I am in harmony with the beloved'. It's already control; simply by imagining that you are different from the beloved.

Q: Is this longing imaginary?

K: The longing is as real as you think you are. The moment you think you are the puppet; the longing is as real as you think. Then that becomes your reality. You are the Almighty and whatever you imagine becomes Reality. If you imagine being a relative puppet, this relative puppet becomes your reality. The only solution to this is to be what you are, not by any action, not by any understanding. Whatever this puppet understands can only be relative and can never bring the puppet out of what is the puppet. It just simply confirms the puppet that needs to understand. That is the mischievous game.

Q: So, being prior to consciousness is another idea?

K: Yes. It's another trap because then you become a puppet who longs for something what is prior.

Q [Another visitor]: And you have been yourself in that trap…

K: That's why I can talk about this bullshit.

Q: You always try to put that puppet down...

K: Why do you still appreciate that bloody puppet? Thinking that one is so important that someone should care about me. I am the most important puppet because there is no more important puppet than me. That is the nature of the puppet – I am so self important and the Self should really take care about me. [Laughter] All the six billion people are interested in themselves. No one is interested in you, they only fake being interested. I talk to my bloody self who thinks he can get out of it. And by thinking he can get out of it, he is in it.

Q [Another visitor]: So it doesn't help if the puppet imagines that it is not a puppet?

K: It is still a puppet that imagines it is not a puppet. [Laughter] It happens many times, it is like I am nothing now. The puppet imagines being nothing. Before I was something, now I am nothing. But even no-thing is one thing too many. For me, you can imagine yourself being a puppet for eternity and it wouldn't change a thing. Now to think that you have to get out of the imagination is another imagination, that's all. Your nature is not more or less imagining you are a puppet or you are God. There is no difference. By your Almighty imagination there is imagination, there is God, and there are all that dream-like things and your nature is not changed by that imagination, that's all.

Q: All the differences are only because you imagine...

K: There will be infinite imagination. You cannot get out of imagination because only by imagining, you realize yourself. The Absolute you are, by imagination becomes 'one' who is imagining it. But already that is imagined by what-you-are. So, what to do? How to get rid of your realization as you realize yourself in imagination? Even trying to get rid of imagination is part of imagination. Even that doesn't make you more or less. Isn't it fun?

Q [Another visitor]: So you are fucked...

K: Basically. You are fucked by yourself. But who cares to be fucked by oneself?

Q [Another visitor]: Enjoy the fuck... [Laughter]

K: Does it matter if you are the absolute fucker, the fucking and the fucked? That you don't understand it is a permanent fuck. That's why the lingam of the Shiva penetrating the yoni out of which all the imaginary children come out. But nothing happens. So, be-what-you-cannot-not-be which is origin of all imaginations of what-you-are. But that you cannot imagine, that you can only be.

But by no imaginary understanding, by no imaginary knowledge, by no imaginary whatever, you can become it. That there can be an imagination, you have to exist first! That there is a possibility of imagination, existence has to be there: that is what you are and out of that, imagining happens. But by no imagining you can become origin of That what is imagination. So, whatever you understand, the understanding and the deep insights, is what? Fun!

Q [Another visitor]: So, stop trying...

K: Even that is an imagination. It's already one-too-many who stops trying. Why do you think Ramana gives you – Who Am I? Because by the first you imagine I, Am and then the world. Then, how to get back to the origin of the 'I'. So, 'Who' drops, 'Am' drops, 'I' drops and you are still That. The origin of the 'I' is prior and beyond what you can imagine. That you cannot not be, so be it!

The other pointer is in deep-deep sleep you are without any imagination and still you exist so that there can be the first 'I' imagination in the morning.

Q: Why does Ramana ask us to do the exercise of Who Am I?

K: Because you went out in an imaginary forgetting and now he tells you that in the imaginary going back, you go back.

Q: But this is not...

K: Nothing happens in the first place. But if you want to do something, you can do that. Try 'Who Am I' but even by that you cannot become who you are.

Q: But then Ramana says it is like the burning of the stick...

K: That's the beauty of it, that it doesn't help; as hard as you try. Maybe in one instant you realize that Thank God it doesn't help because you don't need it.

Q: But now you say, there is a way...

K: Of course. But that way doesn't lead to what-you-are. As in the first place you never left what-you-are, no way will lead you to what-you-are. But if you want to walk in a way, walk the way of 'Who Am I'. But even by that you cannot become what-you-are. But still I tell you, if you want to do something, do that.

Q: For what?

K: For whatever.

Q: I always wondered why Ramana and Nisargadatta gave this technique of Who Am I...

K: Everyone gives that.

Q: Even you?

K: I give this technique to those who I want to get rid of and Ramana did the same. He asked Annamalai to do this technique because he was fed up with his questions. Go and meditate for yourself, ask yourself 'Who Am I' and leave me alone.

Q: Ramana would not do that, he was a nice boy...

K: You really think Absolute Consciousness is nice? Ha...ha...ha... I read one of his stories from Sadhu Om. Ramana sat on an ant hill and the disciples tell him you are killing all the ants. And Ramana said, I asked them to go but they would not listen. [Laughter] He could be quite different.

Q: Ramana was nice...

K: He kills you with a smile.

Q [Another visitor]: Now there is a doubt in my mind that maybe there is a way using the 'Who Am I' technique...

K: Who knows? Maybe when you try to harmonize the butter on your bread you realize. What a shit! Then you try the same with your mind; trying to harmonize your mind. Then maybe you realize, 'What the shit am I doing?' Trying to harmonize something that is already Harmony itself. But you always try to harmonize everything because you suffer by thinking that something is harming you. Then you want to harmonize everything around you. Even by your bloody imagination you need to harmonize everything. Even by the possibility of getting harmed, you have to harmonize everything.

Q: Whatever I say to others, I say it to myself...

K: That is ego-centric bull-shitting oneself. That is love. You become a relative lover to a relative beloved body. Come on! What else can you do? You love your bloody relative ego-centric self.

Q: So, enjoy it?

K: Enjoy? You cannot help yourself. A caring bastard caring about how the bastard is today. How did I sleep today? How am I? How is this 'me' and how is 'you'? How are we? How is 'me', how is 'myself' and how am 'I' today. That's love. That is the highest icon of loving-caring about oneself. Trying to save it from getting harmed. You find yourself in this puppet house and then you think that my puppet has to survive. I want to live forever.

Q: So, you create a life...

K: You establish yourself totally in that relative life simply by that imagination. Then you want to get out of that because you are fed up with the relative life, you hate that relative life. But first you fall in love with that; or the love of the mother who hit you in that by saying – 'This is your pampers don't pee in it. After one year you have to go to the toilet yourself.' That is called conditioning. But who can decide not to do it? Shit happens! You have a mother.

Shit! Then you have a body, another shit. Out of shit, shit happens! So, what to do?

Then you go to a psychotherapist. Then you do family constipation (constellation) [Laughter] I am stuck in my mother. Do I love my mother? Everyone tells me I should love my mother but I don't feel it, something must be wrong with me. We are talking about the sense of humour of existence. How more comic can it get? What is going on? The Absolute Self having a mother and then feeling bad that the absolute self doesn't love the imaginary mother. Then he fights for it.

Q [Laughter]: Imagining the mother, imagining the love and imagining making him unhappy...

K: Imagine! [Laughter] How crazy can it get?

Q [Another visitor]: And the baby is born because?

K: From the relative point of view you have a baby because you want to have sense in life. A ghost needs importance because for a father or mother it is very important for your being. Then you are really someone. Then the baby gets training in the self-importance of a ghost so that it can itself become a ghost.

Q: But when the baby is born it has no ego...

K: And then comes the mother. [Laughter] Then comes love.

Q: It all starts with Adam and Eve?

K: It all starts with Adam. Adam is already dammed. The beginning is Adam and the end is Adam. But prior to the beginning and beyond the end is what-you-are; and even in between you are what-you-are. You are prior, during and beyond that imaginary Adam, what is That and That cannot be obtained by any effort, never be attained by any understanding, never be attained by any meditation, never be attained by whatever you do or don't do.

You can say that you can attain 'I Amness' but you cannot attain That. All of that, by effort or no-effort can be attained as a circumstance but never That what is the origin of all imaginary circumstance.

Q: For trying to be 'I Amness' you have to be aware and that is a lot of effort...

K: For some it's not so bad to go from I Am the body to the 'I Amness'. Even Nisargadatta said in the earlier books that once I believed to be born, there were people. Since I am space-like spirit, the 'I Amness', there are no 'me' or 'others'. That's the difference. Since there is no me, there are no others so it seems comfortable, but it simply means that there is still one there who needs that comfort as he is in discomfort of being an imaginary puppet. Then oneness is better than separation. There is still one who discriminates. For sure for the one who discriminates, oneness is better than separation.

Q: I always meditated where I tried to be aware all the time and it is such a burden. Always judging yesterday I was aware and now I am not aware. It was like a party...

K: There is no guarantee that you do your best and you get the prize. Otherwise imagine one who sits down in awareness twenty hours a day all the time, he would win existence. Imagine existence could be controlled by that; by your action or non-action or your awareness!

Q: For years and years I tried to be aware and I come here for three days and I say... Oh well, who cares! [Laughter]

K: It's fun.

Q [Another visitor]: It's extraordinary to feel this despair that it is a water tight trap; that any doing or non-doing makes the situation worse. Once this trap is seen the only thing possible is to be in this total despair...

K: That's called hopelessness.

Q: And that is your gift...

K: That is what I present. [Laughter] It is the eye of the needle and only when you are absolutely naked, you are gone. And nakedness of existence means there is no hope anymore of any better place or any paradise that you can imagine that would make you better. That is nakedness of existence and by being in that nakedness of existence, you are automatically That. But any idea, any understanding, any whatever you think can give you comfort is controlling. Never will ever any owner go through the needle.

Naked existence is the absolute existence of knowing what-you-are and what-you-are-not. And by that, you are automatically That but not by any imaginary understanding or anything what is yours. That is the heart knot which is the owner knot. It breaks when it breaks. And by that breaking the owner is gone and without that owner there is nothing to own. There is naked existence which is already that what is the origin of whatever you can imagine. But that cannot be done. As much as you want to get rid of the owner, you confirm that bloody owner which is the devil idea that he owns something – my life, my kingdom. So, there's one king too many.

Whatever I do is present the hopelessness, and the only Absolute way out, is that you never were in. Every other hope that there can be an understanding is continuation of ignorance, and ignorance is missing what-you-are. No way out! This is again a trick but only that Absolute hopelessness is the holocaust of the 'I'. It's like a hell-fire, it is a total despair. Only by that absolute despair, the pair drops. There is only despair because there is a pair, there is separation. What to do?

Q [Another visitor]: So, when Nisargadatta gave prescription is it because the resignation didn't happen?

K: I didn't say that.

Q: But when the other teachers give the prescription...

K: When they give it with the hope of helping someone, it is a relative help.

Q: It can be out of a good intention...

K: It is always good intention, that is not the question. But good intention comes out of separation.

Q: Can there be a trick where a teacher knows?

K: No teacher knows. As long as there is a teacher who has something to teach, he has something to learn. Even a good intention needs one who has that good intention. That is always is an intention or a *vasana* that is one-too-many. Even good intention is one intention too much.

Q: And normally they are totally unconscious of that...

K: They have to be. The trick is absolute. You cannot blame them; it has to be like that. But if you believe in them, you just...

I don't blame any of them, they cannot help it. As I am That, how can I blame them? I have fun with myself, that's all.

Q: The trick falls by itself...

K: It doesn't fall, that's the trick. The last hope that maybe one day it may fall. Because they tricked themselves, it is a trickster tricking another trickster.

Q: They trick themselves...

K: Of course! Who else? You still try to imagine a hope that there is someone who in spite of not knowing that he helps, he is helping. What a trick! There is only consciousness tricking itself and nothing happens. You don't have to justify anyone, that's the beauty of it. Neither you nor anyone else has to be justified for anything. That's peace. There is no judgment day; there is no one to judge. There was never anyone who did anything, not even consciousness. Nothing is ever done, nothing ever happens, that is the end of judgment day. The judger would be dropped when it would be dropped but until then it will judge. There will always be a moment in time where there would be judgment, comparison. There will always be a comparison of higher and lower which you cannot get rid of. It will get rid of you, but not by needing it.

There is never any necessity of existence to get rid of you. What kind of existence would it be that has the necessity to get rid of you? That existence no one wants to be. That existence what is worth to be is what-it-is in the presence and absence of any 'you' or any world. And when it drops something, it drops something, but not because of something. It simply drops something. It is like an accident, there is no need for it. So, you may wait forever because there is no need for dropping anyway.

Q: The wait is in spite of wanting to wait or not...

K: You cannot not wait

Q: There is nothing else to do anyway...

K: As you have never done anything, there is nothing else to do. The last trick is that you think you are less and less involved.

Q: Sometimes I see that, sometimes I don't, the trick is very strong...

K: The trick comes out of the Almighty energy of Existence and you cannot go against yourself. You try to exhaust the inexhaustible. The origin is inexhaustible and the trying is inexhaustible both come out of the same origin. That is the hopelessness that I present. Both the tendencies, trying and not trying come out of the same origin. That what has the tendency of embracing and wanting to kill oneself both are inexhaustible. They come out of inexhaustible origin of existence. Both cannot be exhausted, wisdom, love, intelligence, intellect, all is inexhaustible because all in nature is existence. So, even ignorance is inexhaustible because nature in ignorance is knowledge. How can you exhaust ignorance? So be what-you-are in spite but never because.

Q [Another visitor]: Castaneda said hopelessness is too much...

K: It's all too much! If at all, then hopelessness is the gateway for the eye of the needle. And helplessness is your nature. Existence cannot want what it wants before existence wants what it wants. You cannot imagine before you imagine, that's the whole problem, but you try... you want to imagine before whatever comes out of your imagination. You want to control yourself and that is called suffering. That is ignorance.

Q: Sometimes...

K: Sometimes?

Q: Sometimes you want to be out of control...

K: But even that is control. The worst control is wanting not to control. Then you want to control the control. It gets worse and worse I tell you! But you try and try. Keep trying. You are a running out model anyway; this humanity. Once there was a time without humanity and there will be again a time without the bloody humanity. This so-called humanity with all its self-importance is a fleeting disease of existence.

Q [Another visitor]: All the dinosaurs and all what existed before is also consciousness manifesting itself?

K: It is all consciousness manifesting itself.

Q: Stars and the galaxies?

K: The whole theater, the whole circus.

Q [Another visitor]: The best movie ever!

K: It is the only movie ever made, so it has to be the best as you cannot compare it to any other movie. It is the best what can be. The problem starts only when you compare it with another movie. Then you are in shit. When you imagine another movie, then you think that it could have been a better movie. You know what is this sign of infinite?

Q: The number eight (8)...

K: Yes. It is like a twisted zero. If you look at it from the other perspective, it looks like one (1). First there is a 0 and from a different perspective it looks like a 1 and when you bend it a bit it looks like 8, the infinite sign of time. So, it is all a zero. When there is zero, there is awareness, when there is 1 there is no-time, when there is 8 there is infinite time.

Q: When there is a big bang...

K: There was no big bang, there was always zero and you are the zero-zero; the absolute toilet.

Q: So, why do they go on about big bang?

K: Don't ask me. Am I a scientist who is stupid enough to look for that what is science?

Q: So you are saying it was always there?

K: What?

Q: Okay...

K: All ideas. And you still imagine that by understanding that you have some comfort. Maybe for a moment there is a comfort of mind that's all. Then it starts again. Even if you have to remember that understanding, it is already a disease. Even the deepest understanding, the most precious insight makes you an owner of the understanding and immediately you fear to lose it again. Even the owning of awareness is fear. It is all False Evidence Appearing Real.

Q: That is what I was thinking, but curiosity...

K: Curiosity killed the cat. You see the beauty of perfection. It is such a perfect trap. It is perfection itself, even in the trap, in ignorance. It is the perfect ignorance.

Q: And I cannot get out of the perfection...

K: You cannot get out of the perfection you are. And perfection is that there is no second. So, ignorance is in itself perfection as there is no second ignorance. The nature of ignorance is so perfect and you again and again step into the next trap. So what?

But that is the quality of existence. You can step into all the imaginary traps and it has nothing to lose and nothing to gain by the quality of traps and how the trap is.

Q: So, if I feel that I have to go to Tiruvannamalai, it is a trap...

K: Why not? It is exactly what existence wants you to do. Why do you doubt it? You want to control by thinking that even Arunachala is a trap. So what? You think if Arunachala is a trap then I don't go to Arunachala, I go home to Holland. Do you think Holland is not a trap? [Laughter]

Q: So you should do what you do...

K: Just do what you cannot not do. The beauty of what-you-are is that you don't have to love yourself to be yourself. You don't have to like yourself to be what-you-are. I am giving the pointer to freedom, that you don't have to be free to be what-you-are. That you don't need any liking of disliking of any comfort to be That. I am pointing to moksha, to that what is not depending on any control. You think that if you see Tiruvannamalai as a trap then you can control and not go into the trap.

You want to have the absolute sweetness, but you cannot taste that. But you still want to taste it in a relative way. That's the bloody bullshit you try to do. You try to taste yourself in a relative taste. You try to taste the nectar of what-you-are in a relative circumstance. That is your absolute trap that you are stupid enough to fall in love with that; trying to taste the tastelessness of the nectar you are.

Then you take these little bliss moments of sweetness, the pre-tastes... ha...ha...ha... There is no pre-taste of that tastelessness or pre-understanding of that what is knowledge. Thank God! One thinks and claims to have that. The ownership always claims – mine, my understanding, my not-understanding. Then there is a rush for the gold – Klondike. Then you become an alchemist, you want to make gold out of shit. Always hunting the holy grail of everlasting life trying to drink from the nectar of life. Wonderful hope put in to life by religions. And all of that comes from what-you-are. All that imaginary dream coming out of the absolute dreamer you are. But that you cannot imagine. In that imaginary dream you imagine all the wonderful kind of religious ways. Then comes Buddha and tells you that the way is the goal.

You fear the absence of the second so much only to find out that there is nothing. So, nothing happens. Why did Jesus say don't fear what-you-are? But as a ghost, you fear nothing more than the absence of the second.

Q: As a second human being?

K: The second is the second. That there is something else other than you. That's the second. And the split-second is being what-you-are that is splitting the second by being That what-is. That is splitting the second. It is not like splitting something or destroying something. How to split something which is not there? How to destroy that illusionary what...?

Q: I try to hold on to the other illusionary human being...

K: The other is hell. When there are others, its hell. No way out. The instant devil is there, he creates others, because without the others the devil cannot exist. So, how do you get rid of the devil? That's why you have all the techniques of awareness, of vipassana, so that you destroy the second and in the destruction of the second, the one without the second cannot survive. It will automatically be destroyed without a second. That is called Advaita... maybe or maybe not because then even Advaita becomes a concept. But it is a nice one.

Q: I didn't get that...

K: Advaita means no-second, non-duality. In non-duality there is no possibility of the one to survive because one always needs a second. In the absence of the second, there is a total annihilation of the first idea of 'I'. Advaita becomes a concept for the destruction of the first concept and in the destruction of the first concept, both concepts drop.

Q: That is the burning of the stick...

K: That is Ramana's 'Who Am I' or burning of a stick.

Q: But that cannot happen?

K: It will happen when it happens. It is already happening because you are looking for it as the future demands this moment to be as this moment is. Maybe the future demands it that the past can be as it is and not the other way round. Maybe the future creates the past because the future is already there so the past has to be as it is to fulfill the future. So, you now looking for the awareness or the burning of the stick could be because the stick is already burnt in future. So it has already happened, don't worry.

Q: We come back to the same thing...

K: We come back to the same thing that it is not in anyone's hand. So enjoy what is not yours. Who gives a shit about this awareness? Then you always come to this 'me'.

Q: It reminds me of a documentary where scientists argued why the arrow of time cannot be backwards...

K: There is a total interrelation. One cannot be without the other, they are co-dependent. So, who controls what? God and devil, future and past all are co-dependent. One doesn't exist without the other. Who created what? The understanding that future is already there and past is just fulfilling the demand of future is quite relaxing. But it is still an understanding one can have.

Q: They also said that the events in the present can influence the events in the past...

K: Who knows? And who cares? Maybe, maybe not. Does it make existence more or less if it is one way or the other? Everything can be imagined but it still would be an imaginary future or past that can be influenced by each other or not influenced by each other. Who cares about the imaginary present imagining to control the past or the opposite? It needs one who cares. It needs one who wants to know things because when he knows, he thinks he can control.

That is scientific – controlling existence... wanting to know what is existence, what is the origin of existence simply by the fear that otherwise it controls me. So, before it controls me, I want to control it. It is all fear. Fear coming out of the false imaginary evidence that there is a separation, that something happens. Out of that fear you want to go to the beginning because if you know the beginning you control existence and then you are sure that it cannot control you. Always wanting to be the master of existence. Like the devil is the master of time. Sounds good.

Now all the quantum physicists become Buddhists because they now think it is impossible. They say without the observer the particle is sometimes a wave and sometimes a particle. It is always changing depending upon who is looking at it. So, truth is always changing depending upon who is imagining the truth. Then the truth becomes like the one who is imagining it. So, that cannot be the truth. Truth cannot be sometimes in one way and sometimes not, or can it?

Q: [Laughing] Maybe?

K: Maybe truth doesn't have to be constant. Maybe truth can change infinitely and is still the truth and never needs to be a specific truth. Maybe truth as ignorance is fine. No problem for truth to be in the form of ignorance or in the form of wisdom or in the form of love. Maybe truth doesn't give a shit about what it is. Only you give a shit because you want to have truth. And the moment you want to have truth, you are really in the toilet.

The beauty of truth is no one can own truth. So you cannot define truth and truth doesn't need a definer and nothing is finer than the definer as the one who wants to define and wants to make truth finer – awareness, the superior truth.. Ha... ha... ha... Imagine truth would care about superior truth. What kind of truth would it be?

Q: Could there be Avatars who can.... well, that already sounds like an absurd question...

K: Yeah. As if there are two kinds of Avatars, one who could and others who could not.

Q: It seems like Avatars play with this illusion and show us it is all an illusion...

K: No. Consciousness plays an Avatar.

Q: I can see his body has nothing to do with it...

K: It is like a magician, a sorcerer who wants to control existence. Every puja is trying to control the future. It is all magic. Every priest is a magician trying to pray to God trying to make him do things that he wants him to do.

Q: But I can see in case of Sai Baba his body has nothing to do in it. Do you think anyone was tricked in that?

K: No. There was never anyone who was tricked in that. Consciousness doesn't need to be excused to be tricked by something else. It is the trickster, the tricking and that what is tricked. It plays the doer and the victim, it is not different. It is the absolute doer and the absolute victim of that doing and it cannot blame anyone else as it is the absolute origin of the doer, the doing and the victim of that doing. It plays all the roles, Osho, Sai Baba, Karl or anyone.

You can only 'be' consciousness, you cannot have it. That's the beauty of consciousness. So, be-what-you-cannot-not-be which is consciousness, knowledge. And there is no second edition and there is no one ever who owned consciousness. That is moksha. You are that what never can be owned, not even by yourself. There is no ownership in consciousness, never was, never will be. There is a played owner, a played owning and a played owned. A played subject, a played object. A play of Shiva as cosmic consciousness. And you are not different as you are That. You are simply hypnotized by the idea of imaginary others, imagining that you as a seer are different from you as seen. There is a belief system that the seer is different from that what is seen. You are so hypnotized by yourself that you cannot break it. Even by trying to break it, you confirm one who needs to break it.

You have to be what-you-are even in that illusionary hypnotized state.

Q: It seems like the uninterrupted silence is enough anyway...

K: It is always enough, but not for you. It is the ever-present awareness that is always enough. But for who?

Q: But in that there is no one who asks, 'For who?' anymore...

K: It needs one who compares and the one who compares is already imagined. The one who compares himself has no reality. If there is any reality in that one who compares, it should be uninterrupted. It is one of the fleeting shadows of the imaginary, sensational, phenomenal, empty, experiences. So, even the experiencer is an experience. By who? That you will never know but that is what you are.

But any moment you want to know that what is That, you become that what is the relative owner and you cannot avoid that. That is called misery – missing That what never needs to know itself to be itself, simply by wanting to know yourself. But then to realize that in that nothing happens. You can go out or in, imaginary in, imaginary out, and nothing happens for what-you-are. So what? Stupid or not stupid, who cares? No one has to be clever to be what one is. No one has to love oneself to be oneself. You don't have to like yourself to be yourself. You can be the absolute asshole and who cares?

That is freedom for the asshole you are; or the ass you are. But you are not the hole, you are the complete ass. Totality itself that plays many assholes but it is still the ass itself. And sometimes it stinks, so what? Sometimes you are the absolute stinker smelling with your absolute stink. But if you are smelling yourself, who cares? Nisargadatta said if you smell the fart in your blanket, it doesn't matter. Only when there is someone else, you would say 'Oh shit'. It is like being trained how to behave by getting married. It is like in a circus there is a ring master with a beast that has to be trained. Isn't it fun? In marriage first the consciousness is un-behaved, with stinking socks everywhere and then there is a behaved consciousness. A woman comes and says we will work on that. [Laughter] Both played by consciousness and consciousness has fun about it. It even has to believe in that role to play it really nice. Consciousness is the best actor in Hollywood. These are all the roles in that moment and that is Consciousness.

Q: We should be paid for these roles... [Laughter]

K: Being paid by yourself. Sometimes I wonder why don't the Advaita seekers go to the Bank and say give me the money, it's mine anyway. God not thinking about anyone else. Such a powerful trance making people believe that there is only one God, such a powerful trance! Do you think Mr. Hitler otherwise could've done something by his bullshit speaking? He could not even make a good sentence. [Laughter] Because he was Austrian and could not speak good German anyway.

Q: He had problems with his mother...

K: No. He had problem with the professors of the art academy in Vienna and they were Jews. It was a personal revenge.

Q [Another visitor]: When I try to understand, I don't understand anything...

K: And the worst is when you try to get out of it. Then you are really in shit! Even that you cannot, it's like you first fuck and then you try not to fuck.

Q: I just realized that I am scared of being alone...

K: Absolutely! And no one will ever be ready to be alone.

Q: I create the second one which is my ego and I am still scared to be alone...

K: It is all because you fear to be alone.

Q: I fear to be alone, that's why I create the 'I'?

K: Absolutely! Then you try all techniques by going to a cave somewhere to get rid of that fear. But as much as you go to the cave, the world is with you.

Q: Yeah. Then I think it's futile all of that; trying to be alone...

K: Even trying to be independent, because you know it that you cannot be it, you are very safe.

Q: As an ego?

K: Yeah. Constantly you confirm that you want to be independent, that confirms that there is someone else. Even when you want to get rid of the others, you confirm that there are others.

Q: Oh my God, that is so smart!

K: I tell you it's so tricky. Even when you want to get rid of something, you confirm that there is something that is different from something else. That is like in the Life Of Brian when he says 'Leave me alone, let me go home' and people say 'He knows home so he must be the Messiah'. [Laughter] Also when they say 'Everyone is an individual' then he responds 'No, I am not an individual'. Then not becoming an individual becomes more attractive. You only seek what is attractive because not everyone has it.

Q [Another visitor]: Yes, because I want to be special and that's the only reason I come here...

K: Absolutely!

Q: It's not working. Coming here has its advantages and disadvantages...

K: There are advantages but no one has them.

Q: And what about disadvantages?

K: There are disadvantages but no one has them. [Laughter]

Q: Can you give me a disadvantage that I don't have?

K: No one has them. In relative there are infinite disadvantages. If your parents don't have the money then you are in a disadvantage that you have to work. But if you have rich parents then you have the disadvantage that you have to live according to them. The moment you have parents you suffer already.

Q: So there are no real advantages or disadvantages?

K: What is a real advantage?

Q: Real advantage would be not to suffer...

K: No that would still be a disadvantage because then you are depending on not suffering to be what-you-are. Any advantage you can imagine is a disadvantage.

Q: But you used the words 'worth being'...

K: 'Worth being' is being that what never needs any advantage or disadvantage to be what one is.

Q: So there are no real advantages or disadvantages?

K: But that is the Absolute advantage; not to need one. Absolutely no need of anything. That is the nature of what-you-are which never needs anything to be what-it-is. And that what needs any imaginary advantage or disadvantage to prove its existence is an imaginary existence which always needs to prove itself; and im-prove itself. Im-proving is proving itself. So, it's always a proof of a devil and devil already is a fiction, an imaginary idea that the devil needs all the imaginary ideas to survive. The imaginary devil is the 'me' who always needs the other enemies to survive. A 'me' or any 'me', it's all the same. And any 'me' is your enemy; especially the first 'me' is already an enemy.

Q: The devil itself...

K: Yes. Any 'me' is the enemy.

20th June 2007
Ladakh, India

The Absolute Gift Is That What-You-Are Needs Nothing – Not Even 'Nothing'!

∽

Q: I read your book where you talked about relative awareness and awareness which is...

K: Awareness of Awareness. That what is Awareness is with and without awareness. That Awareness which doesn't need to be aware to be aware...where 'my' awareness stops and Awareness 'is'. Then there is no one left who has awareness or is aware. So, the absence of one who is aware, is Awareness. But then he doesn't know Awareness anymore.

Q: Then there is nobody?

K: There was never anybody.

Q: Yesterday you spoke about the 'ghost' Karl, the 'I Amness' Karl and the 'Absolute' Karl...

K: The Absolute in a relative experience, the Absolute in the oneness experience, the Absolute in the awareness experience. But all three are experiences of the Absolute.

Q: For everyone?

K: For the Absolute. The Absolute is now experiencing itself as a Dutch person living in Brussels. That is the relative experience of the Absolute; experiencing itself in a relative way. But it doesn't make the Absolute less Absolute as it already is, or more Absolute. Nothing happens. It is simply the Absolute experiencing itself as a Dutch guy pondering about what the Dutch guy is.

Q: But there is a ghost experience...

K: There is no 'ghost', that's the problem. You want to kick someone out who is not there.

Q: I am trying not to try to kick out...

K: That is too much. So, what is this Dutch guy? He is always one-too-many and one-too-less. Never right – Thank God! Never fits and never has to fit, that's the beauty of it. It is sometimes fitting, sometimes not fitting. But who cares if it is fitting? Who is the fittest?

Even Ramana spoke about seven ways of Self experiencing itself. There are three relative ways and four non-relative ways. The Self in relative experiences and the Self in Absolute experiences which are not different than the Absolute experiences. It is Absolute experiencing itself in a relative or a non-relative way. The first three are: I Am body, a relative experience; I Am the spirit, a relative experience; I am oneness, a relative experience. Then there is the fourth one, which is prior and beyond that what is Life, in spite of anything: that is Absolute – not relative. And from there comes the Absolute not-relative experience of total detachment of being awareness because there is no second to anything. Then Absolute Being 'I Amness' – Absolute, no second. Then being that what is the world – no second.

It starts with relative experience and then it becomes not relative. But even by the relative experiences, nothing happens. They are simply the seven way of the Self experiencing the self. Absolute Existence experiencing itself in seven different ways. Seven different grades of that which is knowledge. And there is only knowledge,

knowledge, knowledge, knowledge... in all of them. So all those experiences are fine.

Q: And all can be realized...

K: Self-realization is the fourth state. That is being prior and beyond all imagination. But it is not something that has to be achieved: Self-realization is the nature of the Self. So, it is nothing new, it is not something that happens. It is simply the realization that what-you-are is never never-realized. It is to be That what is realization itself and not what is different to something else. But that is called Self-realization, Consciousness realizing that it can never realize itself, is that what is realized already.

Q: Where does the deep-deep sleep state fit in to the seven states?

K: It is the fourth state. Absolute not knowing itself. It is an absolute absence of one who is experiencing or not experiencing Self. The Self is that what is the Self without any experience of the Self. That is the deep-deep sleep. That is the nature of knowledge. The Absolute experience of that what-you-are – what-you-cannot-not-be – which is absolutely independent of any experience.

Q: I can understand that it is independent of any experience, but in what sense do we realize that in deep-deep sleep?

K: There is no one who realizes anything, you simply exist – that's all! And existence doesn't need to experience existence to exist. That what is existence Itself doesn't need existence to be that what is existence.

Q: What is the fifth state?

K: In the fifth state, It wakes up, but no one wakes up in that. Then you are the Awareness but no one who is aware. The sixth state is, you are 'I Amness'. The seventh state is, you are the 'World'. The seventh state is like God saying – I Am That I Am. I Am That – I Am; that would be pointing to the seventh grade of knowledge. But the fourth state – *turiya*, is self-realization. It is like an uninterrupted Brahman. Brahman without any interruption, knowing or not-knowing; no one cares. Simply being that what is the Brahman in an absolute absence of one who knows or doesn't know to exist.

Q: I go to that state every night...

K: No one goes there. You are dropped every night and you pop-up every morning, that's all. But no one goes into deep-deep sleep. That is the misunderstanding. You think, 'I go to sleep'. Ha... ha... ha... The idea of 'you' will be dropped every night, that's all. Then Existence remains as Existence, in spite of your idea of Samuel. You think earlier that you enter a state. No. You just get dropped as an idea and what-you-are simply remains as that what-it-is.

Q: Why do I pop up again?

K: Why not?

Q: But why?

K: Because it is a functioning of a self-realization and in this functioning there is an aspect called Samuel which cannot be avoided. Without that aspect of Samuel, the Absolute Self will not be Absolute. The Tao would not be the Tao because without one Samuel in this bloody world, there would not be a Tao.

Q: But in deep-deep sleep, the ego...

K: The ego is dropped. Every night it drops.

Q: But the body...

K: The body is not there, nothing is there. In deep-deep sleep where is the body? Who cares about the body? You have to ask someone else was there any body when I was asleep. Then he says, 'Yes, there was a body'. Then you get second-hand information that confirms that there was a body. Then you are happy.

Q: But you need to make a little effort to maintain this body...

K: Who cares?

Q: But there is a difference...

K: It doesn't make any difference. The deep-deep sleep is here-now. It's not something new. You exist here and now or not? That existence which is here-now is in that deep-deep sleep. Simply know yourself that doesn't need all of that to exist at all. It is not a different state. It is here-now what-you-are. Know yourself as That as you know yourself as that Existence which doesn't need to know itself to exist, that's all! It's not a pointer to your absolute nature and not a different state of happiness. It's here-now or never.

Q [Another visitor]: But you don't know yourself in deep-deep sleep.

K: So what? Do you know yourself now? [Laughter]

Q: I think I do…

K: Bullshit. Bullshitting yourself, that's what you are doing now.

Q: There is a commentary going on inside all the time…

K: It's a trinity of ignorance; this commentary.

Q: Whatever that might be, but it's still not there in deep-deep sleep…

K: What is not there?

Q: This commentary…

K: Who tells you?

Q: I am not aware of it…

K: So, who cares?

Q: You say realize yourself as you realize in deep-deep sleep…

K: Yes. Realize yourself as That what-you-are in deep-deep-sleep because that what-you-are in deep-deep sleep is now that what-you-are.

Q: There's no problem…

K: No problem is still a problem, the one who has no problem. In the beginning you make a mistake by thinking that you need to enter a state like deep-deep sleep. Then you are in spite.

Q: But one enters the deep-deep sleep state...

K: No one enters the deep-deep sleep state. How often do I have to tell you that? But you may still say that enter something, but it is not entering something, it is dropping of something. That's all. You are the Absolute seer here-now that doesn't have to see anything to exist. The scene drops, not the Seer.

Q: The experience drops...

K: Even the experiencer drops and you still are what-you-are. Imagine what you are with and without the bloody experiencer you think you are. You are the lover the loving and the beloved, you are That. So, in spite of the lover, in spite of being in love with the beloved incarnation, you are! That is self-realization; there is nothing more to it. To be That what doesn't need to be or not to be – to be. So, to be or not to be is not the question!

It is simply a pointer to that what-you-are here-now as an Absolute seer looking out of all these eyes looking at infinite different points of view of what is the Self. When it all drops, it is just That. But it is not different to anything.

So, what would you try doing for that?

Q: Nothing...

K: And not doing?

Q: Is too much... [Laughter]

K: It's the paradox, you try to do 'no' thing. It is like wishing for wishlessness. Even the wish for wishlessness is one wish too many. And Thank God, by no wish you can gain that state which is not a state. That's the problem because it's not a state. It's a statelessness of existence. There is no state, there is no circumstance.

Q: So, what about the seven states?

K: Just concepts. But they are not so bad. So, what to do? I like them; they are quite clear showing the seven different ways of experiencing what-you-are. They simply mean who cares in which of the seven states you experience yourself, you just are. As none of them can make you more or less as you are.

Q: The deep-deep sleep state...

K: It's not a state. It's statelessness where all false states appear in. But it is not a state. If it would be a state, it would be a state in something else. Any state needs a circumstance; a state in a state in a state. The moment that you try to imagine it, you are bala-bala.

Q: So, what am I doing here?

K: Are you here?

Q: Apparently so...

K: Because you had a parent, you are apparently here? [Laughter] Because my mother told me.

Q: I don't remember that...

K: But she gave you her tits, that's enough. You became a sucker by that anyway; wanting more. Every seeker starts by sucking a tit.

Q: It is always that little bit more that you want, that you can't quite get...

K: Then if mother's tit does not satisfy, then you look for a universal tit in the spiritual bullshit – God's tit. You even create a mother out of God.

Q: It is more complicated to reach the tit of God...

K: That's why it's called a bra-man. [Laughter] It's tricky because the moment anyone tells you deep-deep sleep is your nature; you immediately ask how can I reach that? Even if Ramana tells you 'be what you are', you ask 'How'? How can I be what I am? This 'how' you cannot get rid of. How did you do? Tell me your secret. What's your biography of entering the *turiya* state?

When Oneness happens, it is dropping of separation. It is not like someone entering oneness. That's all. The Awareness is already there, the I Amness is there and then there is a separation experience. If you sit in oneness for twenty years in front of a wall in *zazen*, then suddenly the wall drops and you and the wall are one. It's not because you enter a different state. It's just that separation experience drops in a way and 'I Amness' remains. So, Oneness was already there. It is not something new.

So, no one enters oneness. It is simply like the separation experience drops and oneness remains. Then the oneness drops and awareness remains. Every night that happens, first the world drops, then oneness drops. Then in deep-deep sleep even the awareness drops. Then you are in the Absolute darkness of your Absolute existence. Neither knowing nor not knowing if you exist. Then every morning there is popping up of Awareness, I Amness and then the world. So, nothing happens.

You are here-now in that experience of separation That what is in oneness or in Awareness or in absence. Because without the Absolute seer you are, there would be no seer, seen, what can be seen. So, nothing new.

Q [Another visitor]: The fifth, sixth and seventh state...

K: They are not states; they are ways of experiencing yourself. There are relative ways and non-relative ways.

Q: Ramana said...

K: Ramana never said anything. [Laughter]

Q: Consciousness or prior to consciousness...

K: Is an imagination! Even prior to consciousness, you imagine. But that there can be an imaginary 'prior' to consciousness, by still trying to be prior, you have to exist. That there can be an imaginary idea of being prior, you have to exist. That there can be an imaginary idea of separate world, you have to exist. That there can be an imaginary idea of oneness, you have to exist. That there can be an imaginary idea of awareness, an experience, you have to exist. In all that state, you exist. That existence never changes in all the different experiences. So, there are differences, but by all the differences, nothing is changed.

Even if you try to deny Existence, you have to exist. So, what? That you cannot get rid of; that's your nature, Existence itself! Without that existence, there is not a slightest imaginary idea possible. So, even the seven grades can be there only as an idea because you exist. You are the origin of all whatever can be imagined, but you cannot imagine to be That.

Q: It's now 'me' trying to imagine...

K: You try to imagine That. And by trying to become that, you become that what is an imaginary existence. And by that imaginary existence, you miss yourself.

Q: Is that what 'I' do?

K: No. That creates a 'me' who is missing itself. The Almighty Absolute Brahman imagining himself as something and by the Almighty imagination gives reality to a shadow. Then by being the shadow, missing what it is. How stupid can it get? Then trying to imagine a better state. I can always point out; you have to be here That what-you-are, which is Absolute Existence. Whatever comes in future cannot make you more or less as That. No imaginary state can ever deliver that what is an imagination. There will never be any image. Thank God they are all empty. Empty promises that one day you may know yourself. And by that promise missing yourself permanently; permanently pro-missing. Missing myself and then being in a misery of missing.

Q: Now I am grabbing on those seven things...

K: So what? For me it doesn't matter. You can grab your underwear, who cares? [Laughter] Do you really think I would care? Or existence would care? So, have fun with the seven states.

Q: How come this information is there? Is it just to fuck me up?

K: Of course! All that is made by yourself to fuck yourself.

Q [Another visitor]: That is called an insight... [Laughter]

K: He still takes it personally that someone made it for him. Why is all that bullshit there? Because you are, you made all that bullshit but you just forgot it. You are the origin of all that bullshit. This is one hand clapping. [Hitting on forehead] It's 'me'. No one else to blame. No God, no guru, no underwear, no mother to blame for anything. All the mothers are because you are. The Almighty Self pitying itself and complaining why is this all here.

The origin of whatever can be or not be is complaining why there is anything at all. Poor me! Now I have to make this body in order. It's an infinite job. Every night it falls down and every morning you have to put it back in order. [Laughter] Looking at the mirror – Ah, you again! Every night you go to bed and say – If I don't see you tomorrow morning, it was nice to meet you. Every morning – Ah, you again! Shit!

Without saying absolute goodbye every night, you could not even sleep. There is an absolute goodbye to the world. Without that absolute dropping of the world, you cannot even sleep. It's an automatic dropping of all ideas.

Q: Dreaming is also an imagination...

K: That is like you picking up ideas again.

Q: What is deep sleep and deep-deep sleep?

K: Deep sleep has a dreamer; deep-deep sleep is without the dreamer. It is That what is the dreamer without the experience of the dreamer. That's why they say when you need the Samadhi of awareness, you don't go out of the flow of energy or awareness. It's like permanent awareness day and night. But it is still making a difference between the permanent and the impermanent.

Q [Another visitor]: What is meant by keeping quiet?

K: You repeat something what no one said. It is – be quiet and see.

Q: How to be quiet?

K: How not to be quiet? Try not to be quiet. That's the problem, you cannot not be quiet.

Q: It doesn't always feel so quiet...

K: But that there is something that is not quiet, you have to be quiet because there has to be difference between something which is not quiet and something that is quiet. So, first there has to be something that is quiet so that there can be something what is not quiet. So, what's the problem?

Q: I am lost...

K: I hope so.

Q [Another visitor]: It is more a description than a prescription...

K: It just describes your nature. No, it is not a remedy for anything. It's not a Ramana remedy. It is not a remedy for becoming what-you-are. It's always a paradox. They always tell you try 'Who Am I?' and the next sentence they say, 'But by all of that you cannot attain what-you-are. But you have to try. The self-inquiry may never stop. So, you have to become Mick Jagger anyway. I can't get no satisfaction; but I try. [Laughter] That's all there is.

Consciousness cannot not try to know Consciousness because in that trying it realizes itself. Realization of consciousness is consciousness meditating about that what is consciousness. That meditating consciousness will never stop. The meditation is the nature of consciousness. The only problem for the one who is here is that consciousness became a meditator expecting something out of meditation. It became a worker. It started to work on itself. That's called masturbation and not meditation.

Meditation is your nature and you became a meditator expecting something out of that action of consciousness. That makes you suffer about not being able to gain it with your action. In that sense expectation is hell, misery. 'Me' is only there when there is a meditator expecting something out of his doing, his understanding. All of that comes out of his so-called action. As consciousness realizing that by all of that, nothing happens, that is the realization of Consciousness becoming meditation again, where there is no meditator meditating about anything. Without expectation there is no meditator.

So, there is realization of consciousness, but it's still relative. Then there is oneness of the meditation but it always falls back to a meditator expecting something, so it's fleeting, fragile. Many people say by that awakening, now I feel so fragile, I have to keep it, I have to polish this understanding of consciousness because very easily you are out of it again. So, it cannot be it. Existence cannot be fragile – come on. Who has to keep that state? Anyone who has a natural state, even defining the state of existence, what can it be? It needs a nature and a not-nature, definer and not-definer. So, there is a fine and define, not-so-fine state. So, who wants to be awake here in that fragile state of awakening? Then making all the effort to stay there...

Q [Another visitor]: So, the three states are just an exploration of consciousness, rather than getting something out of it?

K: This trinity is realization of Reality and there are three different forms of meditation. There is a meditation in the world, as a meditator expecting that by his doing something comes out of it. Then comes the oneness, no-meditation where there is an absence of a meditator, there is non-identification. There is absence of identification but there is still a realizer who is identified in oneness. This is the way Reality is realizing itself, in trouble and not in trouble.

The creator is already created – by what? What is the origin of the creator creating what can be created? The meditator meditating in whatever way, what is its origin? It is deep-deep sleep which is origin of deep sleep which is the awareness state, then the 'I Amness' state, just starts to dream, then what can be dreamt of all relative forms. Prior and beyond of that is what is That. It's with and without.

Q: What is the point of all these guys telling us to go back to the awareness?

K: Because they speak from there. They landed there and they can only speak from the point they landed. There was one who landed in awareness or one who landed in oneness. It's like a teacher in a school landing as a teacher of algebra who tells you about mathematics. He tells you that you have to learn mathematics in life because you may need it someday. Then comes the oneness teacher who experienced oneness. For him everything is oneness; no separation. Then he speaks from oneness. That is his reality. When even that drops, then he speaks out of awareness, out of the Light. I am the origin of everything, because of me everything is. I am aware that I am that origin which is Lght which realizes itself as form and non-form. You cannot blame them. For them it is absolutely their reality.

The self in those three states becomes the reality based on where you give attention to it. If the self gives attention to awareness, it becomes awareness. When the self gives attention to I Amness, it becomes the I Amness. When the self gives attention to the world, it becomes the world. When it gives attention to the body, it becomes the body. It falls in love with first with the body, then it becomes the body. Then it falls in love with oneness and it sticks there. So, three different ways. But does existence get more or less by that? Does the quality change?

That's why the Upanishads say if there is a teacher who has something to teach, he has something to learn. The teacher has to be dropped and the jñani who knows a jñani is one jñani too many. Even a jñani is one too many. God knowing himself is one God too many because God knowing himself is always two God's. It's an instant, if God becomes aware, it needs two Gods. One God who becomes aware about God, that's already two God's. Oh God, Oh God!

It starts innocent, falling in love with itself. Then it becomes an imagination of innocence. God falling in love with the idea of God creating a second God; me, myself and I. Then God is in trouble because he forgets that by his imagination he created a second God. Then the imagination suddenly becomes reality and then he wants to know the second God or know himself, both are not different. There is an imagination that he needs to know himself to be himself. What to do?

Q: Can one speak from world or I Amness...

K: You can speak from wherever you give your attention to. If I speak about astrology, I speak from the relative world.

Q: Where do you speak from?

K: There no one speaks, that's the problem. There is no speaker, no speaking, nothing is spoken. No one is listening and nothing is here. This is what it means by – nothing ever happened. Even in that so-called blah, blah, blah; nothing happens. It is just energy in action, but nothing happens. There is an absolute action; and the reaction is not different. The absolute action is reacting to itself. So the action and reaction is not different because that what is acting and reacting is not different. So, nothing happens.

The doer and the victim are not different. Both are played by energy that you may call consciousness or God or whatever. But even prior to that is That what is God. That what I am becomes a dream of chain reaction of action-reaction of consciousness which is the karma of consciousness. This karma no one has. Even that you may call a dream. Consciousness is already a dream because That what is consciousness doesn't know any consciousness – never needs to know or to be conscious or unconscious or aware or anything. All that is dream.

That is the deep-deep sleep pointer. Know yourself as That what never has to know anything; not even Itself to be what-it-is. Consciousness is already an idea because it has to exist to be consciousness but that Existence you are doesn't even have to exist to exist. But don't think you have to go there because you cannot go there.

Awareness is a guillotine, cutting whatever can be cut and being the absolute cutter that can never cut itself. You are the absolute counter and that's the only thing what counts. But whatever you can count, you cannot be. You can count the world, you can count oneness, you can count awareness. It's all countable. But you cannot count the counter. But without the counter, there would be no counting and nothing could be counted. Even the counter you can count is not the counter. But that what is the counter is the only thing that counts.

You never count yourself. You always count what can be counted but never count the counter. Without the absolute pre-sense of the counter, there cannot be an experience of the counter, the experience of I Amness and no experience of the world. It's so easy to be but so heavy to become. It's impossible to become but impossible not to be. Even you trying to become makes no difference because you are anyway what-you-are.

But the only difference is that you are in the misery of imagining that you can be found and I sit here and tell you – be happy that you cannot find yourself, my goodness! Every finding is hell. Hellelujah!

Q [Another visitor]: I have to say, it's a relief...

K: Being the absolute relief of not being a leaf on the tree of concepts. It's quite a re-leaf being what-you-are and not being a be-leaf system of the tree of bullshit.

Q: I agree because I always want to count the leaves on the tree of bullshit...

K: A leaf wants to become the origin of the leaf. Imagine! How can a cup become that what is the cup? It's already the cup. I want to know the cup, says the cup. I want to know that what is the cup. It's like a cup wants to capitulate or devote something.

Q [Another visitor]: You say that sit here and do nothing...

K: I don't say that.

Q: So what do you say?

K: I say be what-you-cannot-not-be.

Q: I don't get it…

K: And you are not here to get anything.

Q: I'm here to get something…

K: But I'm not here to give you anything. That's the biggest gift you can get.

Q: Then why are you here?

K: I have no idea. You tell me, I am always waiting for someone to tell me why I am here. No. what I can only present is that what I am doesn't have to know anything. It doesn't even have to know to be here or not. So, there is a total carelessness of being here or not. But you care about why I am here and why you are here because you want to gain something. I can only present that again and again, there's nothing to gain. You are the gainer who has nothing to gain.

I can only point to the absolute gift that nothing can be given to you and what-you-are never needs anything. It needs no gift at all to be what-it-is. So, what's the point? No idea. But that for me is the absolute gift. Simply presenting the absolute gift that what-you-are needs nothing, nothing, nothing, to be what-it-is – not even nothing. No presence of idea of any imaginary understanding or insights or anything to be what-it-is.

Q: It's best to give up…

K: No. Even that is too much work. First find what is yours and then we can talk about what you can give up. No, this is devotion of the devoter. It's not for understanding. You cannot have understanding here and take something home and work with it. Imagine someone imagines that you have to work and then something would come out of it. Imagine always questioning yourself – 'To whom did it happen? Is this really real?' No. I like chaos.

Q [Another visitor]: A real punk...

K: I used to play in a punk bank in the late 70s. I am the absolute punk. It's all rubbish anyway, so who cares?

Q: Can you talk about your biography? [Laughter]

K: Now you go too far.

Q: Come on, we have time...

K: There is no time for biography.

Q: A little bit, in five minutes...

K: There was this day on 12th of December on 1953. It was very heavy for my mother in 4o' clock in the morning because I was nearly 10 pounds. She was pressing and pressing and it was very impressive for me because I didn't want to come out. [Laughter] Then there was a tunnel view and a light was coming in and it looked very promising and I thought it was the end of the tunnel. So I pushed a bit towards the light. Then I got hit [bang] and I realized, I am wrong again. [Laughter]

Then from the first day, I was laying in my glory, lying naked on my bed. Then a nurse came and a pee came out directly towards her. I was back in business. Pee where you are, that was my exercise. My biography starts with 'Pee where you are'. That exercise we all have in common as a baby. Then comes your mother and tells you, it's not good – I will teach you not to pee in your nappies because I don't like to wash them. You have to take care about your bloody body. Oh, that again! [Laughter]

So, it took one year and then I could walk and found the toilet. [Laughter] Then people coming and making faces in front of you and I thought – Are they stupid? [Laughter] Do I really want to grow up if I have to look like them? But you cannot help yourself. Then you are hungry and you see light coming out of a big ball and you suck on it few times in a day. You live only for that. Do you want to continue the biography of Karl? [Laughter]

Q: It is like a movie...

K: It is like a movie. It starts innocent and then you grow a little older and say – Oh, my goodness. It's hell from the beginning. Back in business, having a body and needing to feed this bloody thing. When you get three years old your brain starts to be hungry for the sensational bullshit of learning. Then someone teaches you how to create a knot in your bloody shoes. From that moment you think – Who wants to be reborn? Never again. I want to stop the wheel of reincarnation. [Laughter] So it goes...

That reminds you of how this idea started that you don't want to come back again. If you don't like your mother, you create an idea of God where you don't have the body to take care. Freedom – free from body, free from dependency. It always starts like this. No difference. Even God Rama needed to be taught that all this is a dream and nothing ever happened.

This started becoming real when you started to believe in it. Then you started to get more and more into this gross body experience; crossed by gross body – crucified. Then you become a spiritual seeker. Then you try having a relationship with your girlfriend because you think when you are one with someone, you are out of the business. Ha... ha... ha... Relation shit happens. [Laughter]

What do you want to know?

Q: About being a punk...

K: We had a band called WC – water closet. Playing in front of three thousand and not finding any note. And the people liked it, they like you as you are. Just having fun and they have fun; that's what I'm doing here. That's art. You have no technique, you cannot play anything, you just be there and everyone is enjoying. That's fun. That really gets you out of the business that you really have to produce something or present a defined music. While painting I do the same, no difference.

Just be as you are – whatever comes. The moment you try to impress people and you want to do something so that they love you, they question you. Then they question you – this is not so good. Then you question yourself. Then you really become a pain. The moment you become an artist who is waiting for a response from people, my goodness. Help me God!

In that way, punk is fantastic! No response needed. You are just out of your mind, playing whatever comes out energetically like fuck you all... and they like it. This is not a love song; it is a pill for everyone. And everyone relaxes in it – I don't need this bloody love. If at all, the best that can happen is you don't even have to like yourself to be what-you-are. You don't have to love yourself. You don't even have to love yourself. You can hate yourself, you can like yourself, it really doesn't matter. Who cares? This is really relaxing – I don't have to like myself to be myself. Fantastic! I can be the absolute asshole and who cares?

What is moksha? What is freedom? It is the carelessness of existence. Being that what never needs anything to be what it is and not trying to be a good artist so that everyone likes you – bullshit. Really fuck it all! You are fucked anyway from the beginning. You come out of a mother mother-fucking fucking... [Laughter] Then you really imagine that something can come out of that? Excuse my language, but it's not mine. [Laughter] I'm trained in Australia.

Q [Another visitor]: Is your biography important to reach to the point where grace drops this...

K: Every bloody moment. You cannot say what is important and what is not. You will never know. It's always unique. There is no comparison in it. Milking cows and being a good boy or being on peyote everyday in a different reality and being a bad boy. You cannot say what is good or what is bad. It's just... whatever.

Q: So what happens when Grace comes?

K: Grace never comes, that's the problem.

Q: So, how would you put it?

K: The joke is Grace is sitting here now and waiting for Grace. Your nature is Grace itself and what-you-are is waiting for Grace to happen. Can there be a bigger joke? That what is knowledge waits for knowledge to happen. Knowledge is here-now that absolute Existence which can never be more or less as it is. Existence is waiting for Existence to happen or what?

Q: I'm asking you...

K: I tell you, Grace never happens.

Q: The parts of your biography where you had and it felt like an absolute rape from existence, you didn't tell me about those...

K: If grace is after grace, grace cannot find grace. But if grace is after you, you will be dropped as nothing – that's all. When grace is after grace, then watch out. But even that is may be...

Q: So, there was an experience of waking up...

K: Many! Many waking ups and many going to sleep again. Every night I go to sleep and every morning I wake up. Every morning there is an awakening. Oh 'you' again!

What would be the nature of the awakening that is worth being?

Q: I don't know...

K: Can it be worth being what comes and goes? Experience of awakening happening to a fleeting shadow. Who cares about the awakening of a phantom who wakes up to a phantom life; from relative to non-relative life. Who cares about an imaginary 'I' who wakes up to what? From what?

Q: So, nothing happened?

K: It's an infinite happening but by that infinite happening nothing happens. So, happy, happy. That's called a happening. An absolute happening and by that happening nothing happens. That's fun, that's entertainment. Entertainment in which nothing really happens. It's like a Hollywood movie.

And I tell you, the best thing is there was never anyone who walked this earth ever woke up to anything. There was never anyone who walked this earth who was enlightened. That's the best that can happen to you. To see absolutely that there was never anyone who realized That what is reality and you will not be the first one. That is called peace; peace from mind.

Q: It is a very peaceful concept...

K: Too full or too empty? But that's the pointer from Buddha. What to do? [Pointing to a visitor] Imagine there would be a Dutch Buddha. If he would get it, no one else can ever get it anymore. He would be so stingy that he would only share it for a moment.

Q [Another visitor]: There are people who think they are realized...

K: Let them think. It's like a banana – a banana realization. There is a banana who imagines to be realized. It's all a Ramana banana. Imagine there could be one who is realized! Then you say I want it too. Then you become greedy that he got it. The very idea that there is one who got it, that there was an Osho who got something, that there was Ramana who was realized, that there was Jesus or Buddha or whatever, all that is hell. That feeds your idea of enlightenment and you become a monkey by that. A monkey who thinks by getting a banana he would be a happy monkey. Happy ever after, having the ultimate banana. Having a never ending banana.

The monkey mind becomes a greedy bastard for that absolute banana. It's amazing how they catch monkeys. They put a banana in a jar and the monkey tries to get it. But in the process he cannot get out of it. They catch the monkey just by its greed. Every seeker is like that – caught by that banana. [Mocking] I'm holding on to enlightenment. I'm sitting here, trying to let go. This trap is so infinite because you think that without the banana, you are hungry because you are so greedy for that bloody banana. You want to know yourself, so you hang-on. Then suddenly maybe the banana disappears, then you look for it again and find it.

It is like they say in Zen Buddhism. You sit in front of a wall for twenty years and suddenly you are gone and relaxed in oneness. Then you say, it has to be mine, I want to have it, I want to stay in it. [Bang] Back in the banana-business. I want the bloody banana; I don't go home without a banana. Maybe I should wait until the banana is rotten. But then it doesn't taste anymore. So I want it now – with the power of now – not later. [Laughter] Maybe if I just stay in the moment, maybe I can reach the banana – that's choiceless banana. [Laughter]

Q [Another visitor]: Then maybe you have to go beyond the banana... [Laughter]

K: Then there is one who comes and says you have to go deeper. You can do better. There will be a deeper banana. [Laughter] There will be an omnipotence of the banana. Then you become greedy for the omnipotence of existence.

But I tell you, God is absolutely impotent. He has no potency; he doesn't even have a dick. That is absolute omnipotence but absolutely impotent. It cannot even want what he wants. What kind of God is that? Imagine! But that kind of God is what you are. A God who cannot even want what he wants. Being the Almighty, energy itself. It cannot want what it wants. What impotence.

But you imagine that when I am that Avatar, I'm into the omnipotence of existence. Then I can do what I want. Ha ha ha... Then I will control everything. With the blink of an eye, I can be everywhere like a genie, but I don't know where I want to be. Shit! Now we're talking about omnipotence. Going to a homeopathy to purify your existence, wanting to be healthy, wanting to be holy. Holy shit!

All the doctors tell you, you have to purify your so-called body. Get active, get healthy – and you buy it because it promises you to be a healthy seeker. Then you have more time to seek. [Laughter]

Maybe you have a hundred-and-twenty years and when you are hundred-and-nineteen, you get it. [Laughter] What to do?

There is a joke about the carelessness of God. When Titanic hit the iceberg and it was sinking, there was total chaos in the ship. Then one person goes to the priest of the ship and tells him – Please go to your boss and ask him, maybe he can do something. So many people are dying. The priest closes his eyes for few moments and then opens them. The person asks – So what did God say? The priest replies – God is busy right now, he is playing battle ship.

And you expect God has time to come and help you? Imagine what kind of God would that be who has to help you! I tell you, God doesn't even know you! What kind of God would it be who knows you? I would not like to meet that guy who knows you or even himself. Who wants to meet a God that knows himself? What kind of God would it be who comes down and helps someone in his despair? A pitiful God? You have to pity him so that he can pity someone else. First he has to pity himself so that he can then pity someone else. What pitiful God do you expect to help you? Or Grace... what pitiful grace would it be that pities you?

Be happy that there is no help from any grace or God or anything. Be happy that you are not something that needs to be helped at all. It's all a joke, an infinite joke. If you don't start to laugh, then you are in a serious business.

Q [Another visitor]: What about happiness?

K: I like it. [Laughter] What kind of happiness would it be that you can have; which would be your happiness? Imagine there would be someone who can have happiness – 'my' happiness.

Q: Peace?

K: No. That would be hell because then there would be someone who has peace and everyone else would be jealous about it. Then you have to buy it from him because he doesn't want to share it. That would be really Dutch, selling happiness. Then you sell milligrams of totality – like hashish. [Laughter] Imagine you would have peace, you would fear to lose it again. Imagine you could gain happiness which would be your happiness, then you fear that one day it would be gone again. So, even in the happiness that you can own, there is unhappiness because you can already imagine that one day it would be gone again. When you experience, immediately you imagine that it would be gone tomorrow. It's so fragile. And you already fear that. So, there is no happiness in happiness. It's still unhappiness.

Whatever you can own, whatever you can gain, whatever you can have, there is a fear of losing it. So, it's already unhappy. I would just forget happiness and be what-you-are, which doesn't know and doesn't need to be happy to be what-it-is. That you may call the happiness 'you are'. But that happiness is not something you can own. So, it will not be your happiness anyway. Forget the idea of happiness; forget the idea of God, truth – if you can. Drop the dropper, drop the dropping and be what-you-cannot-not-be. In that there is silence, which is peace itself which never needs anything to be what-it-is. And nothing else other than being what-you-are would make you absolutely satisfied.

Nothing else, not any relative idea of happiness or unhappiness or salvation or whatever you can imagine can make you satisfied. Only to be Sat itself, satisfaction itself; and that is never-never. Never needs more or less of any kind of imaginary bullshit experience of whatever you can experience.

Be what you cannot not be and that is happiness itself, that doesn't know any happiness and doesn't own happiness. It is happiness, it is knowledge. But it cannot be owned by anyone – neither by yourself or anyone else. Your so-called Buddha nature never went out of anything. You are the shyest of the shy. You never showed up. What-you-are never showed up as anything.

Q [Another visitor]: What about sadness?

K: If you are sadness itself, there is no one who is sad. When you are that what is ignorance, there is no one who is ignorant. If you are that which is whatever, you are That; and in That there is no suffering. Only by your having it, there is a sufferer. The owner is the sufferer, the ownership is suffering. The Absolute ownership is being what-is. In that there is no second and without a second, there is no possibility of suffering. That's why it's called as Advaita. Advaita is the absence of the second edition of existence and without a second edition of existence, there is no existence that can suffer about itself. For suffering, it needs two – one existence suffering about the second existence, that's all.

Q: For the relative happiness, does it need two?

K: For unhappiness, which is relative happiness, it needs two. It needs one who can be happy or unhappy. The relative knower, whatever he knows is relative knowledge. And relative knowledge cannot satisfy that what is Knowledge. And only to be that what is Knowledge is the satisfaction of knowledge.

Q: Then there is here-now?

K: There is no here-now, that is the problem. That what is the here-now, doesn't know any here-now and doesn't have to be here-now to be what-it-is. So, even the here-now becomes a concept because if there's a here-now then you ask, what is not here-now? Or to be in the power of the bloody 'now'. Then you always ask yourself this question – Am I now in the bloody now or am I now in the bloody later? [Laughter] Or how was I before? Was I in the bloody now before or am I now in the 'now'?

You better don't know what-you-are at all, or what-you-are-not. Any moment you know what-you-are in the circumstance, you are missing yourself. There is a misery underlying everything. So, what to do? It is a 'me'-sery.

Q [Another visitor]: I'm losing all my friends...

K: The good thing about losing all your friends is that you lose all your enemies too. This is the split-second, when the idea of ownership drops, you lose friends, enemies. You lose the story of whole existence.

Q: You want me to feel sorry that you lost all your friends?

K: Me? No. I tell you be happy if that happens. That is what you are looking for – losing all your friends. Especially losing the one who can have friends. That's the worst, being the potential one who can have friends. At the moment you are any 'me', you are your own enemy already. Any 'me' is your enemy I tell you, again and again. Specially the 'me' who needs friends makes enemies just by confirming the one who can have enemies.

Q: What to do?

K: Have some Dutch help. [Laughter] There will always be one ready to help you asking – How can I help you?

Q [Another visitor]: How come the teachers who are in awareness don't know?

K: How can they know? It is absolutely as it has to be.

Q: Yes, but why?

K: Why asking why? It is as it is.

Q: By teaching from there, is it possible to drop?

K: No one is dropped there, that's the problem. The dropper gets dropped.

Q: Why teaching from that space?

K: Consciousness is stupid to teach anything at all. Any teaching is stupid enough – even to start teaching. Doesn't matter from where you teach. Teaching already is too much. It's an idea anyway – dreamlike teacher, dreamlike teaching and dreamlike being taught. Who cares from what position stupidity comes? [Laughter] It can only be ignorance, be happy. Whatever position the teaching happens from, is ignorance. Be happy that knowledge cannot be known by anyone and cannot be taught and truth cannot be given or taken away from anyone. Truth cannot be owned by anyone. So, whoever is teaching, from whatever point, is ignorance. Hallelujah! Thank God and praise the Lord!

Be happy that they teach from awareness. Be happy that no one teaches from knowledge. Again and again I say that be happy that what-you-are cannot be given or taken or taught – never needs to be taught to be what-it-is. That what needs to be taught what-it-is, will find one. One stupid finds another stupid. Like two enlightened persons meeting and exchanging their techniques – How are you enlightened?

Q: There must be a 'me' who they want to help...

K: It needs one who sees others. Only when there is one in self-pity, he sees others and wants to help others. It's all pitiful. Whichever teacher you find, is a pitiful teacher in a pitiful self trying to help other selves. The blind trying to lead the blind – that's all. Unlimited ignorance. What to do?

And I don't say here it is something else. I can only present ignorance because that what is knowledge cannot be presented, that's all. And I'm absolutely happy that That what is knowledge cannot be presented to anyone – not even to myself. It would never be present to anyone. There would never be anyone who is the president of the Presence, one who is in choiceless awareness. And then teaching out of that choiceless awareness. I tell you there is no teacher and there is nothing to teach – but that I teach you.

Q: Why can relative ignorance be presented but relative knowledge cannot?

K: Because relative knowledge is ignorance. And you can never get satisfied by relative existence or knowledge. All cannot deliver what-you-are. Knowledge is your nature and you never lost that what-you-are and you cannot gain it back by anything. So, be happy that it cannot be found and given by anyone, and no one can have it. Whatever is – is That. But no one can ever own That. There is no ownership in all of that. Ownership is the only dream. The owner-cheat – the cheater cheating himself. Then being unhappy that he doesn't have enough; a greedy bastard who suffers about not having enough. Oh my goodness! A phantom owner suffering about not having enough phantom ideas. Sounds good.

So, you better don't wake up – when you wake up. Don't wake up when awakening happens. Every morning there is awakening, but who wakes up? Your existence is already there, so nothing happens. In the beginning nothing happens and in the end nothing happens. That's the whole teaching of Buddha. Look the divine accident happens every morning; the divine accident that the Absolute existence became aware of existence. But that Absolute existence was prior and beyond the awareness what-it-is. It never needed this awareness; but shit happens. It woke up! And that is called the divine accident. Accident means even the absolute existence cannot avoid waking up. It happened. Did something happen? No! Your nature is still what-it-is in spite of being awake or not awake. It's not so bad – it's worse. [Laughter]

You are really a donkey when you believe in the carrot. This wouldn't last, the moment you step out of here, you would forget it anyway. That's the good thing about it. You don't have to remember anything what is said here to be what-you-are. Isn't it fun? It's all absolutely irrelevant and entertainment. Irrelevance of talking, irrelevance of listening. There is no need to talk, no need to listen, no necessity of anything. But still it happens. And you cannot avoid it – just see that it cannot be avoided so enjoy it. But any moment you want to avoid it, you suffer by trying to avoid yourself – isn't it crazy? Because this is an automatic realization of Reality and by you trying to avoid yourself, you suffer.

Be that what is the Reality and in That realizing itself, That has no beginning and no end. So, enjoy yourself because it will take a while. Infinite while? Maybe or maybe not. But who knows about how long it takes? Even infinite is not long enough.

Papaji said you are in the transit lounge of existence. You are waiting for your next plane but still you want to make your own house, your bedroom, your toilet. It has to be yours and it has to be as you like it. All this, just being in the transit lounge of existence. Departing anyway and you cannot take anything with you – all your bloody gold and bullshit shoes. But you buy anyway. [Laughter]

Q [Another visitor]: You never had any physical guru...

K: [Sobbing Jokingly] No. I had to do all by myself. [Laughter]

Q [Another visitor]: But it was not so bad...

K: When it's done by the Self, you can be assured that it's well-done – with or without master.

23rd June 2007
Ladakh, India

Hope Is For The Spiritual Kindergarten, To Make The Kids Quiet

∽

Q: Yesterday you spoke about the brain surgery experiment. What was that?

K: It was a proof that no one has a free will.

Q: How so?

K: They put some electrodes in the brain which made the person do something but he still claimed that he did it. But it was proven that the impulse didn't come from him. The external influence made a person do something but he immediately took the doership or the responsibility for the action of the body. It was a reaction but the reaction comes after the action.

Q [Another visitor]: There's another scientific experiment which proved that the impulse to act came much later than the thought came.

K: It's all an independent movement, independent of what you want or not. But you are able to take it over immediately after and you do as if you have done it. If 'you' could accept that, there would be no you anymore because there would be no story of 'your' action. That would be the Absolute non-doership because you cannot find the doer anymore. That's the basis of Ramesh's teaching. It's all God's will but there's no one who did anything.

Q [Another visitor]: Is there any difference between your sleeping and waking state?

K: Yes. Now I see you, that's called hell. [Laughter] When I sleep, I don't see you anymore. There are differences, but they don't make one! What's the problem with differences?

Q [Another visitor]: Yesterday we talked about paradoxes...

K: Yes and No. It's all yes and no.

Q: Can you elaborate on that?

K: I'm not here for work. If you have a question, I will answer. I'm not a teacher. I'm not here to make a speech.

Q: As you say... [Laughter]

K: [Laughing] The main thing is that in dream, yes, but in reality, no! Whatever you say is in the dream, there's an impact of whatever that can be done or not done, but it stays in the dream. So, yes in the dream but no for what-you-are. There will never be anything in the dream that you can do to attain what-you-are.

So, yes you can do something but by all of that you cannot attain what-you-are. Yes, you can do, but no it wouldn't help you to become what-you-are: that's why yes and no. And you have to do something anyway. So, do it, but don't expect that you can attain yourself by that. That's called meditation. That's action without intention, there's action without expectation of a fruit later. That's already quite peaceful. Anything else is not meditation, its just work – expecting to be paid later. Then you're just a slave of a future goal and a future payment of some God who pays you for what you've done or not done. That makes you this little slave who needs to be paid later and greedy for more payment.

Q: I think you said something different yesterday...

K: I always say something different, that's nothing new.

Q: That's the paradox...

K: It's not a paradox. I don't want to bore myself by always saying the same thing. [Laughter] I would rather say the opposite. If it's true or not, I really give a shit.

Q [Another visitor]: We learn that we always need something to produce something else. But when we sit with you, it seems everything just exists...

K: In dream you work and you get paid for it. In dream it's all fine.

Q: But otherwise it just exists?

K: Don't even bother to know if it exists or not. For that what you are looking for, it's worthless. You will not find peace in that. It will not pay you with what you're looking for. It can never make you satisfied. Whatever you do, it will not give you that satisfaction you're looking for. There's no peace in it.

So, yes you get paid but not by that what you want. You work your ass off for happiness but happiness doesn't come out of it. You do everything, you have a family, you work, you have kids all to own the happiness. Everyone is very selfish, works for his own happiness but it doesn't work. You collect everything, do everything for happiness. But it's never enough. And everyone has that experience, the moment you got it, it's completely empty. Then you have another goal. Spiritual goal is enlightenment that keeps you running. The donkey keeps working and meditating. Big carrot – this enlightenment idea. By that you rot in hell!

So, what to do? Do your best but don't expect anything to come out of it. Then it's already meditation. But how to do that? [Laughing] You would do it for peace and then peace would become a relative object again. Because then you think that now you don't expect anything anymore but then there should be peace at least. So, you again expect something by not expecting something.

Q: It's a vicious circle...

K: It's just as good or bad as anything. It's another trap – from now on I accept everything. Ha, ha, ha. But you expect to get some peace out of it. Loving what is, ha, ha, ha. There are so many books coming from Byron Katie. She's the ninth most influential spiritual teacher of the world. I'm not even listed in the first thousand! [Laughter]

Q [Another visitor]: Why?

K: Because I don't sell more books. It's all about selling books.

Q [Another visitor]: Because you don't give hope...

K: I don't even give no-hope.

Q: That's the reason you're not in the best-seller...

K: I'm before the one, I'm the zero. [Laughter] Hope is for the spiritual kindergarten, to make the kids quiet. [Laughter] Like you learn in school, you learn for life. If you learn well then you become something, make money, have good wife. Everyone hopes to get older and get something but when they reach that age and get it; they say I shouldn't have listened to anyone, it's all bullshit anyway.

No. It's all this hope is for spiritual kindergarten.

Q [Another visitor]: Hope is torture because you can never be at peace. You're always looking for something...

K: No one can be at peace anyway. It doesn't matter actually. Hope is like you want to control somebody. You want to give something to someone so that he runs in a particular direction. It's like controlling someone and giving him a tendency.

Q [Another visitor]: One realizes this game very well but what should one do with their children?

K: Kill them right away! [Laughter] Then the problem is over or kill yourself. You want to have a solution, I give you one. [Laughter] Nisargadatta said that there was a time I believed that I existed and was a householder having a family. Then I was surrounded by six billion people. But the moment I saw that all of that is fake, there was no householder, no me, no other. With that the whole universe disappeared. So, where is the question of family? Just be what-you-are then there's no doctor who has any family or wife. So, kill yourself in that way. The rest is just a junkie who wants to have a better fix.

Q: Till that time, what to do? [Laughter]

K: Just add some *bhang* in your chai. [Laughter] The *diksha* people in Madras they do it every day to thousands of people. Every day in chai there's *bhang*.

You try to be an example for someone, look I'm a doctor, I have a family and I should be happy. You always have to smile in front of your kids because if you tell them all was bad, even having you didn't mean anything. [Laughter] If you're really honest with them what would you tell them? Fuck you all?

Q: So, what should we tell them?

K: Be honest and they'll go by themselves. I had so much hope that with you I would be at least a little bit happy and content but it didn't work. I'm still sitting in Bombay and asking someone what to do? [Laughter] Nothing works.

If you ask me, just be honest. Just tell them that my life is as fucked as yours. Don't take me as an example. If you do, look what comes out of it. [Laughter] But bhang helps too. [Laughter]

Q [Another visitor]: Yesterday you mentioned that in Bhakti you cannot say 'I surrender', it just happens...

K: Grace takes everything away and then you claim that you gave it away.

Q: What is a better way? Bhakti or jñani way?

K: Both are equal. At the end the jñani becomes a bhakta with dropping of jñana and bhakta becomes jñani by dropping of bhakti.

Q: So, bhakti would be much simpler...

K: No. You don't know how much you have to donate. [Laughter] No, you have no choice. Whatever is meant for you; by understanding, you give up everything, or by giving up everything you understand both are no different. The energy of that understanding comes when nothing belongs to you anymore, then there's a natural understanding. Or you have a natural understanding that nothing belongs to you anyway, but both come together, there is no two. Bhakti and jñani are not different in nature. For jñani even the knower dropped. So, he gives up knowledge and is that what doesn't even know what is knowledge or not. It cannot happen by understanding or by giving something. Both doesn't work. Both are futile but in that futility, it drops by itself. As it cannot make you what-you-are, it drops by being what-you-are and that can only be done by grace anyway.

So, jñani and bhakti is Grace and when it drops, it drops but not because you want to drop it or you want to devote something. You will never be devoted enough. You devote only because you expect something: and you want to understand because you expect something. Both is expectation. Both don't work but because they don't work, they work!

It's like Buddha trying for forty years and not making it. Then there was a split second that nothing ever worked and nothing will ever work to know oneself. Then he is Buddha but it doesn't mean that he becomes a Buddha. He didn't become a Buddha by whatever; his Buddha-nature was already there. He was just giving attention to something false. The false drops when you see that the false is false. But the false can never make you that what you're longing for: all understanding and all devotion is false. Ramana calls it the devotion of devotion, the renunciation of renunciation.

Being what-you-are is renouncing the renouncer because you can never renounce yourself: you are That. You can never give something because nothing belongs to you. All of that points to That what is your so-called divine, superior nature. So, what to do? Making a difference between both, is mind trying to find 'What's a better way and what is my way?'. You still believe that you can do it your way. Then you think am I a bhakti type or a jñani type? What am I? [Laughing] Then you do family constipation.

Q: That's where the question came from. If I'm a bhakti-type, I don't have to run anymore...

K: [Joking] I'm a bhakti type and I will only bake cakes. I'm a house-wife, I will get it by baking cakes. [Laughter] Being a house-wife is quite a bhakti. You cook everyday and after a while you really don't expect that someone would say anything. [Laughter] That's a house-wife. After a while you don't cook out of love anymore but just because you have to. And everyone eats not out of love, they just eat. [Laughter] That's called self service. You had an imagination that you would have kids and you would cook and everyone would be so happy, I would have a sense in life, a reason to exist. And all of that's just... [Blowing in the wind]

Q [Another visitor]: Sometimes I discuss this subject with my family and I always feel superior. But when you talk here I don't feel that you're superior. Why this difference?

K: Because you talk out of second-hand understanding. Then you have to prove it, you have to build up authority. You need to have a higher position. But if you are the authority, there's no need of any higher or lower. Then there's just 'I' to 'I' and there's no teaching and there's no one who feels superior to someone else. If you talk out of second-hand understanding, you have to blow it up; you have to make it higher than something else. Because you care about what you say and that people should understand you.

Q: Then even they look up to you as an intellectual...

K: Yes, you are.

Q: It's very dangerous...

K: Just be generous, blow it up! It will explode sooner or later anyway. [Laughter] But you can see many teachers when they speak, their ego is blown up and they're levitating like a balloon. So much hot air inside. But after a while they don't believe you anymore. They listen to you but will not take it for long. Then they fight with you and then you're in trouble.

Q: They already don't take it... [Laughter]

K: You want to save the world or your family. With good intention you try to give them something. It never works. No one wants it from you. In that sense I don't give anything here. What's your purpose for talking? Just see if there's any resistance or just see if you can even resist it or not.

Q: In my case there's a point to prove but in your case there's no point to prove...

K: Yeah. You want to break the ignorance. You want to bring some light into the darkness. I have absolutely no interest in that. This is pure entertainment.

Q: And we still keep coming back...

K: Yeah. I talk to smaller and larger crowds and they still keep coming back. But if you ask them why, they don't know. So, there's already a tendency of not knowing but still things happen. It's always the same story. Many don't want to come here anymore. They're watching the television at home half an hour before the talks and then they watch themselves going to the talk. They're sure five minutes before that they don't go to this bloody Karl, he always says the same thing and there's nothing to get out of it. Then they watch themselves going and sitting. This exercise I like, the exercise of helplessness. That in spite of you getting or not getting anything, totality places you somewhere you like to be or you don't like to be.

If you ask this person Karl, I would never come to Bombay. I would never sit in front of some miserable seekers, if you ask in that dream side of the story. There's a tendency of Karl, of what he likes to do. There are workers hammering outside, this is not Karl's idea of life. But he's just clever enough not to resist existence, so he's in peace with it. He knows he cannot do anything anyway. It will happen in spite of his liking it or not. It is all in spite of your liking or not liking. It will happen anyway. It's not as if I have to accept it: it will happen anyway.

Q: It's just like you cannot pre-think your thought...

K: Yeah, but if you ask me what I would plan, this would not be part of my plan! [Laughter] Honestly. I would never talk again with anybody if you ask me. I tell everyone if you had a choice you would never wake up again from deep-deep sleep. From the beginning you can just fuck it all, this whole dream. There where there's no one happy or unhappy is such a most blissful absence. Then this starts again.

So, I don't just talk about this [Pointing to himself] one. I talk about everyone, for whole existence, for God. If he would have a choice not to know God, he would instantly kill God. But as he cannot kill God, as there is no God to kill... In that sense I say, shit happens but what to do? You don't need it but it happens anyway. You don't wish for it, you have no intention to experience it but you experience it anyway. So, you cannot avoid to dream yourself. This dream is unavoidable. So, it's okay!

Buddha wanted to bring peace and happiness to this world when he saw unhappiness and misery everywhere, then he saw that it will never end. Nisargadatta calls this as an ocean of discomfort, which is a dream. A dream of separation will always be a discomfortable experience. Any moment you experience yourself is an experience of two: you cannot make it comfortable. The more you want to make it comfortable, it's discomfortable. You better give a shit about comfort or discomfort, being in spite of it and seeing that whatever can be done or not done will not end that discomfort. So, what?

In that moment you end as the one who tries. That's all. The seeking of a way out drops because there was never any seeker anyway. The seeking continues without a seeker, without expectation. So, there's still an inquiry without hoping to get anything out of it. If you want to make a difference between being identified with the dream and not being identified with the dream then this is the only thing I can point to. Be established in the Absolute, fuck it all. Or you're fucked anyway. And you're the fucker, the fucking and the fucked if you like it or not.

That's the nature of I Am That because you're the fucker the fucking and the fucked. That's fucked. So, you fuck it all! I don't mean that you stay somewhere where no one is. No, you fuck it all, because you're the Absolute fucker, the Absolute fucking and the Absolute fucked. You're the lingam, the space and the whole dream. The lingam of light, the vagina of space and all that comes out of it. You're the presence of the light, the absence of light and the vibration of light that vibrates as the whole existence. So, you fuck it all anyway because you're the Absolute fucker and you're fucking yourself. Who else is there to fuck? It's an imaginary fuck but it's an imaginary fucking yourself. So, you can call it real or not real, it doesn't matter. It's a real imaginary fuck. And you cannot stop it because trying to stop it is another art of fucking. I just make it drastic because sometimes it resonates more. So, what to do?

Be what you cannot not be. Fuck what you cannot not fuck – yourself. But who cares about being fucked by oneself? If it's imaginary or not, it's always being fucked by oneself – in whatever way. If you complain about something, you can only complain to yourself. Today it was not so good. [Laughing] The main thing is there's no second and whatever happens, you are That. And there's as much happiness as unhappiness in that: it's all balanced. There's as much misery as bliss in anything.

Q [Another visitor]: What reincarnates? A thought?

K: No, energy.

Q: But thought is energy...

K: No. Thought is already information of energy. Information doesn't reincarnate, energy shows itself as different information but it doesn't reincarnate in that information. Life always lives itself differently. You can call it reincarnation of that what is life. But the thought already is one incarnation and the next thought is another incarnation of life. But there's no thinker in it. You cannot find the thinker because the thinker is already a thought, like information of life. Information of life cannot produce another information of life. There's no creator in it. The creator is already an information of life, creating is an information of life, and what can be created is already an information of life. Already the creator is created by life.

Q: And consciousness cannot create a new life?

K: Consciousness can never create anything. It shows itself as a thought, but the thought in nature is consciousness. When there's a thinker, its just Consciousness presenting itself as a thinker but the thinker never has any thought, the thinker is already information. Then you think that the thought comes from the thinker doesn't come out of the thinker, it comes out of the same origin. The origin of the thinker is Consciousness, the nature of thought is Consciousness and all whatever reactions come out of it. So, all the reactions are reactions of energy or consciousness. There are all reactions but not that what is the action. The action is what-you-are but you can never experience the action. What you can experience is a reaction of what-you-are but not what-you-are. Even 'I' the creator – Brahma, is already a reaction of that action itself.

Q: How does every bit of information come from?

K: It is in-form-ation. Like a flower comes from seed and seed came from something else. Then suddenly there's a flower. But where does it start?

Q: The seed is a particular kind of...

K: No. Seed is already produced by a cluster of information of energy. Then out of the cluster is the information of genetic conditioning which is called a flower. Flower is already built in the seed but the seed is already built in the potential of life.

Q: From potentiality comes everything...

K: That's the Absolute potential. From the Absolute potential all that you can imagine appears. But the easiest thing is seeing it as an Absolute Dreamer. An Absolute Dreamer with a potential of all possible dreams. All the information, all what you can imagine, all what you can experience, all the reactions are dream reactions. It's like a dream: a dream you have a dream universe, dream cities. When you wake up, they don't exist. Like here. You can only say that there can be a city, that there can be a universe, that there can be something, you have to be That what is dreaming it or experiencing it.

In the end goes the substratum. You take away everything away, the information, the form, the non-form and even the creator drops. Then you remain as what-you-are what you can call as Absolute Soul which is dreaming itself as infinite different souls or informations.

Q [Another visitor]: There is no free will?

K: There is, as an experience, but not as 'real'.

Q: I don't make any choices at all?

K: There's an experience of a chooser, there's an experience of wanting something, there's an experience of will or no-will or anything. But, as I said, the chooser, the choosing, and what is chosen, is played by That what is energy – call it whatever. So, how can that what is already played have a free will? In that sense you can say it's all a will of God or your will because you are That what is God. But you cannot want what you want, that's your problem. Not even God can want what he wants.

Even the Almighty has no power to change his dream because for changing the dream there should be two. Then the Almighty should be different from the dream. It needs a controller who is different from what he's controlling. But as there's no difference between the Absolute Dreamer and the dream, in nature they are

That what they are. There's no two. So, there's no way of controlling anything. There's a dream of control but it's a dream control, there's no reality in it. In that sense, you control absolutely the dreamer, the dreaming, what can be dreamt. But you cannot control how you control because you are That. You control the totality by being the totality. But there's no right and wrong in you, there's no direction. How can you then know what you want to do if there's no one who wants anything? So, what to do?

Q: It's very frustrating – no free will, no choice...

K: One would be frustrated and another one would be ecstatic – no free will, I can do whatever I want. [Laughter] No free will would mean that you can do whatever you want because it's not what you want. But you can still do whatever you want. Paradox. [Laughter] Whatever you want comes true but you cannot want what you want. That's the whole problem. And not always what you want is what you'd like to want. Then you have a problem.

Q: There's a saying that if you will for something very strongly, you get it...

K: Okay. If you want to be an American, be an American. [Laughter]

Q: I can get an American passport...

K: Getting a passport is not being an American. Try to become an Eskimo, they don't even have passports. [Laughter] If you really really want...

Q [Another visitor]: Then in next life he'll be reincarnated as an Eskimo...

K: What he is is already an Eskimo. [Laughter]

Q [Another visitor]: My parents said if you really have a strong will, then it becomes God's will...

K: It's already God's will anyway. But sometimes you will and the neighbor gets it. [Laughter]

Q [Another visitor]: That's what happened with my father. He wanted a son like our neighbor...

K: And the neighbor would want a daughter like you. The Indian way of solving this problem is having an arranged marriage. That's the way you can get the neighbor's son or daughter in your family. [Laughter] Consciousness doesn't mind. It can wish something in one person and another person gets it. So, consciousness always gets it but not always where it wants it. Every wish of the totality gets fulfilled but not always from where the wish came from. You wish it but someone else gets it. [Laughter] It's like you want to get enlightenment but the neighbor gets it and he really doesn't know what to do with it. [Laughter] Then he ends up in a mad house. I always look around and ask myself, who fucking asked for this one?! [Laughter] You sit in a car which you really don't want. You wanted a Ferrari next door but you have to drive your little Volkswagen.

But if you are what-you-are then you see yourself driving every car, being married with every woman. That's not so nice but... [Laughter] Now it goes too far! You're the prisoner and the guard, then you're always imprisoned by yourself. No way out of it. Who can take that? As a person you cannot take that. As what-you-are there's no problem by being it. There's nothing to take, you're already That. But the one who wants to realize that or to be that, gets frustrated, depressed. Even by understanding that you're all the misery of the world, all the war. What is this world? A place of what? Monsters. It's a hell. Whatever happens in this world, in the families, rapes and all of that? If you look at it like a person, you can really get really down. Now you just have a technique of not seeing it anymore. You watch the news but it doesn't touch you. But if you really would have an open heart towards all of that, there's no enjoyment in it. Then you slowly close your heart again if you don't want to be crazy by it. No one can take that from a reference point of a relative person.

This pity for yourself, seeing the other person as you. Even recognizing that you're everyone and everybody and seeing what you do to yourself. For that you could kill yourself right away for what you're doing to yourself everywhere, even inside yourself. It's unbearable. You can only bear it by being what-you-are because that has no good and bad. Nothing ever happened in that. No one was ever born, nothing will ever die. There's just That what-you-are and it can never be harmed by itself. So, there's no harm in what-you-are.

But you cannot take it from a relative reference point. Impossible! If you're this little human and have these little human feelings, it kills you. That's why many people in this path get quite depressed. They realize that they are not different from all of that. But they still see the happenings and want to change all of that. They have good intention to help everyone. They want to save every dog on the street. If you go to Tiruvannamalai, you would see men with bags of food for the dogs. They're seeing misery in all the creatures. They try really hard but get totally exhausted by all of that. It doesn't seem to work because you see more and more.

Q: Did the separation happen somewhere along the line?

K: [Laughing] You are not online.

Q: In the Bible they talk about the Adam being separate from God...

K: Adam is already separation. When God experiences itself as Adam, the archetype of man – Awareness. When God knows himself, that's Adam – the alpha and the omega – already there is a separation in that experience. Then comes Eve, evolution, life. Eve means Life, the mother of creation. Adam and Eve are not man and woman. It's the male principle and the female principle, the lingam and the yoni, as the cosmic consciousness and the awareness of the superior light and space. Then starts creation.

But already the light is not That what is the superior: already there, the dream started. The realization happens in separation. Even the experience of light, being the lingam, is already an experience of separation. But it doesn't separate anyone. So, it doesn't start there. Then the cosmic yoni and the vibration of the information's is just a realization of the Reality you are. It's an experience of separation. You can only experience yourself in a dream of separation, but you don't get separated by that. There's no separation in that; there's an experience, but no reality in that.

But if you ask where it starts, it starts very early. It's the first, and the last, Adam or awareness, or the experience of light. Already, there, the dream of separation starts. But what-you-are doesn't start there. You are already before that. Prior to the experience of light, you are That what is the light. So, the first experience of light is already a separate experience of light. Then there are already two lights. Even the experience of light is not the nature of light. So, the light of Shiva is not Shiva. Shiva cannot know himself in his own light. It's already second-hand. He will never experience himself as first-hand in any way. You can only experience or realize yourself in second-hand experiences – as an experiencer. But the experiencer is not what-you-are, the experiencing is not what-you-are and what you can experience is not what-you-are. But in that way you realize yourself – as a creator, creating, what can be created.

But all of that is not what-you-are. You are the Heart of That, realizing itself as that. So, it's not different from you but you're not the father, you're not the spirit and you're not the son. You're That what is Heart. But Heart doesn't know any heart. And there's no ownership in that Heart. Heart is heart by being Heart, but no one owns it. Nothing ever happened for that what is Heart. Heart has no judgment about anything, there's no good and bad. There's no idea of how it has to be. No concept at all of how it has to be or not to be.

I ask you to be what-you-are who doesn't know what is good or bad... who absolutely doesn't know what is right or wrong. Who absolutely doesn't know what it is and what it is not. Then its your natural state, this Absolute not knowing at all of what-you-are and what-you-are-not. But any moment you know yourself as anything, you're fucked. Because from that moment on, from that reference point, there will be separation in Reality. Then you want a better realization. Then God wants to have more love in life and then he's fucked, the moment he knows good and bad, he's fucked by good and he's fucked by bad. Its a bad fuck!

Knowing yourself is hell and not knowing yourself is paradise: there are two sides of the coin, the paradise and the hell. The absence of knowing what-you-are and the presence of knowing what-you-are and what-you-are-not. And you cannot avoid any of that. You will always fall in love again and you will identify something with the body. Fuck it all! Then this whole thing starts again. No way out. If one person realizes himself, what about all the other forms and informations? So, maybe God doesn't mind being fucked by himself. Being identified with a person doesn't make him a person. It's just dream identification and doesn't make him more or less in anyway, because he has no idea about what is good or bad. So, even that doesn't have to drop.

I'm just pointing to your nature, which never knows what it is and what it is not. Who never has any idea of good and bad, who is absolutely blind about all of that – the Absolute blindness for anything – by just being that what is. It's not as if someone realizes that and from that moment it becomes the not-knowing. It is already the Absolute not-knowing and not by understanding it or by any technique or by any power of now or something or power of later. Now is later!

So, my dears. Deers are for shooting. [Laughter]

Q [Another visitor]: I was contemplating on the 'me' with the Absolute as the reference point...

K: Make the Absolute absence as your reference point or be in-no-sense, That what can never sense your Absolute reference point. I promise you there will be an instant drop of stories. If you ask me that would be the Absolute way out of all what you can ever sense, whatever you can make a story. Just have the Absolute identification with the superior divine Absolute Being which can never be sensed, even by itself. That's called in-no-sense(innocence). Whatever you can sense, just sense it but don't be it. The sensor you can sense, the sensing you can sense and what can be sensed you can sense. But not what is sensing the sensor. That is in-no-sense.

But the first sensational experience is the sensor, then the sensing, and then what can be sensed. But already the sensor is a sensation, but what-you-are is not. That is the ultimate what neither is nor is not because you cannot say that it is or is not, because you have no fucking idea of what it is and what it is not. But that is what-you-are. You are not a concept. You are not something what can be sensed. How can That what can never be sensed, be altered into anything? It will never be changed by anything because that what is not a sensation will never change his nature. That nature itself is Absolute, That what is in-no-sense. But the nature you can sense, you can call it a dream nature. But the Absolute Seer cannot be seen; it's never part of the scenery.

If that is your Absolute identification, and I tell you That is what-you-are, in That there were never any problems you can drop. Because for That there was never any problem in anything. So, there's nothing to renounce, there's nothing you can devote. That's Ramana's devotion of devotion. By just being That you renounce the renouncer – Absolutely. You renounce renunciation because there is no one to renounce anything. There's a satisfaction beyond your imagination – always was, always will be. This is a direct pointer to That but no one can give it to you. This what is not a sensation cannot be given by sensations – by any *shaktipat*, by any *diksha*, by whatever you can come up with. This cannot be transmitted by anyone, through anyone. There's no transmission possible. I just talk you to That but there's no transmission possible. You are already That. What is here and what is there, there's no difference in nature. So, I can no way help you to be That, I can just point to That.

In that sense I have no interest in taking any misunderstanding away. Every understanding whatever you can understand, comes from a sensational misunderstanding in that sense. Because you can sense it, you can put it in your pocket.

Q [Another visitor]: Nisargadatta said he is in spite of consciousness. I didn't understand that...

K: In one of the books Nisargadatta said, 'In spite of me not needing Consciousness, I cannot get rid of it'. There is no need for the Absolute ultimate to know itself. It cannot not start knowing itself again. It cannot not realize itself as Consciousness. Beyond or prior to Consciousness, Absolute is. But it cannot stop it, it cannot get rid of it, because that's the way it realizes itself, as the Absolute Reality realizing itself as Consciousness.

Q: What did he mean by in spite?

K: You're always 'in spite' of Consciousness but you cannot get rid of the dream. Consciousness is like a dream you cannot kill because you cannot kill a dream. All this imaginary realization you cannot get rid of, because there's nothing. If there really would be a consciousness, there would be a reality in consciousness and you could kill it. Shiva could then kill the light of Shiva. But as there's nothing, there's nothing to hold onto. It's just a dream consciousness and you cannot get rid of it.

If there really would be some substance in Consciousness, if there really would be some reality, you could kill it. By your Almighty nature, you can kill whatever can be killed. But you cannot kill what is not there. So, already Consciousness is an imaginary sensation.

Q: When he says 'I Am That', what does he mean?

K: 'I Am That' is pointing to that Reality which is always prior or in spite; always with and without. He never points to consciousness by that. He said, in spite of me not needing Consciousness, which is just a dream-like sensational dream of whatever you call it, I cannot get rid of it. It cannot be destroyed because it has no own reality. If there really would be Consciousness as a separate reality, maybe you could kill it or destroy it. But even Consciousness is like a phantom, like a mirage and you cannot kill a mirage. It's a me-rage. Consciousness is like the 'me' you cannot get rid of, as much as you rage about it. That's why I always say, 'What to do?' You tried everything to get rid of it but you cannot get rid of what is not there.

The *Parabrahman*, the Ultimate Reality is the only reality which is: there's no other reality! Then that Reality starts to dream itself, out of the blue. Then how to get rid of that? The Ultimate Reality is not part of the dream, so it cannot even act in the dream. It has nothing to do with the dream: the dream is dreaming itself. Consciousness is playing with itself infinitely but there's no substance of a player. It's just an imaginary consciousness playing imaginary players in an imaginary play. So, you better be what-you-are in spite of it. But don't expect that you can get rid of it because if you expect to get rid of it, you make it real. How can you get rid of what is not even there in reality?

So, no way out. Whatever you try doesn't work. And everyone tried a lot! All the siddhi masters, all the Almighty Avatars, all tried very hard to destroy that what is never there. You can only destroy that by seeing it as it is, as a mirage. Then who needs to destroy it? There's Consciousness, so what? What to do with it? No need to do anything with it; just be that what-you-are. Then there's no 'then' – never was! Buddha tried it; they all tried to destroy that. All whatever they called as misery, this ocean of pain. But it's a mirage pain; it's an imaginary universe, an imaginary consciousness, imaginary pain, imaginary discomfort. How can you get rid of the imaginary... whatever? No way!

As I said, if I could help it, I would not sit here and talk at all. Why should one experience itself as someone at all? But if it happens anyway and it doesn't make me more or less as I am anyway, so what? I rather enjoy it, not knowing what it is or not. So, there's not even a need now to know what it is and what it is not. Even calling it play is too much: that's why Silence is your nature. 'Be quiet and see' means be That what is always Silence, never moves at all, and whatever you can see, especially the seer, is already an imagination. It's bad, but what to do?

Nothing ever compares to you, but this is a dream of comparing, always comes in pairs, and you cannot get rid of it. This is the way this consciousness plays; always in good and bad, light and darkness and all of that. But what-you-are is neither. That's why *neti-neti* – you're neither light nor darkness or anything. You're always That and this is the closest pointer, just to call as That and not have a name or anything, just being That! There's no hook in it, no hook for any story in it. There's not even a 'now' in it, not anything that you can say. Nothing clings on you and you don't cling to anyone or anything. That's what he pointed to.

Q [Another visitor]: What is the difference between consciousness and awareness?

K: There's no distinction. How can awareness be different from consciousness? I don't make any distinction. Consciousness shows itself as three different forms – as awareness, as I Amness and as this information of bodies. It's all consciousness.

Q [Another visitor]: Is there a possibility that existence will ever stop realizing itself?

K: As I said before, it cannot stop. One cannot stop what never started, that's the problem. If there would be a dream that started, then there would be a reality in that dream because there would be something what started. But, as nothing started in starting, nothing ends in ending. So, if nothing ends, nothing was there in the first place. But the dream which never came, cannot go.

Q: It's complicated...

K: It's not complicated.

Q [Another visitor]: They say it stops for a while and restarts again...

K: Every night it stops.

Q: But that is for the individual. What about totality?

K: How can it stop? If you think it can stop, you make it real again. Then it would be like a movie which is a real movie.

Q [Another visitor]: Can we say that the Absolute is real and Consciousness is unreal?

K: You can say, but its bullshit too! [Laughter] If you say consciousness is unreal, you make it real; then it exists because even to be unreal, it has to exist. If you say it is not, it has to be to be not. Whatever you say about consciousness makes it real. If you say there's no consciousness, you make it real. You better be quiet, but be what-you-are. [Laughter]

Q [Another visitor]: In siddha yoga they say all is real...

K: It's better that one is quiet than all is real. [Laughter] It's quite heavy because it means that my neighbor is also real! [Laughter] Who can take that? There's more peace in being That what doesn't even know what is and what is not real: where there's no idea of real or unreal because That is what-you-are. In what-you-are there's no fucking idea about anything. But the moment you say something, it's too late anyway. The moment you say it's real or unreal; you're fucked by the real or unreal, no way out! The moment you pronounce it, there's a pronouncer; one who claims to know. Just get established in the in-no-sense(innocence) which is your very nature. And who needs to know what the rest is? It cannot make you more or less anyway. If it's real or unreal who gives a fuck? Who needs to know?

When you really look for peace, there's peace. When you're That what-you-are what never needs to know if it's real or not real, because there's no need for anything. That's why you call it Sat; satisfaction by nature. There's peace by nature but not by any understanding or anything what you can claim. If you ask me, that's the only peace that's unshakable. Nothing can be done with it, no one can own it, no one can give it, no one can take it. There's no quantity of peace. For me that's the only quality I talk about – the quality of what-you-are and not any understanding of quantity of real or unreal.

Be that what cannot be either taken or given by anyone, not even by yourself and never needs to understand anything – not even that! The pointers of deep-deep sleep point to in-no-sense, where there's no sensor and nothing can be sensed in anything. And still you are That. Then this experience starts by itself and ends by itself.

Q [Another visitor]: In certain situations don't you feel that it should change?

K: I always want a change. There's always wanting. It's never right. There's always something that needs to be changed. I don't accept anything, I hate everything. There's an unconditional hate every moment I exist. That's why I always tell people that I hate you anyway.

Q [Another visitor]: We love you too...

K: That's quite relaxing if I say I hate you anyway, you're free to do whatever you like. If I say I love you then you already imagine how you have to behave so that I still love you tomorrow. It's a prison. If I tell you, I hate you anyway, then you can relax and laugh. Whatever you do or don't do is good. Total acceptance in 'I hate you anyway'. If I tell you 'I love you', then you're already imprisoned. You're already thinking how I have to behave. It's like a marriage – I will take care of you the rest of my life and then already the prison is closing in front of you. [Laughter] From that moment on you hate everything. I love you forever – Oh, oh! In good and in bad times – Oh, oh! [Laughter]

Who can take that burden? What love can survive that? You already put everything on top of it. It's like a ship which is already overloaded, it will sink. It cannot survive, it cannot run anymore. Then you wait for your retirement so that you get your pension and the kids go away from the house so that you can be free anymore.

Q: All the bachelors should not get married anymore...

K: They're not better off. They imagine that being married is not so bad. None of that is better. The grass is always greener on the other side. Then you want to cross the river. Then you meet ferrymen who say I can take you. Like a guru comes and you tell him I want a peaceful mind. Then the guru says, I can take you to that shore, follow me. Then he leads you to the other shore and you sit there and think – shit, it was not so bad where I came from. [Laughter] There's nothing here, no friends. Then there comes another guru who says go with the flow, be in the river. Then comes Osho and you say I accept everything. This river can take me to the ocean. But after a while it gets really hard to swim all the time because you wait for the ocean to come but the river never ends. [Laughter] Then there comes the next guru who says the river is already the ocean. Just relax and drown into yourself. Then you drown and ask yourself, what now? Maybe I better go back where I started.

No there's no better place. You will never find any peace in any of that. Not in the other shore, not in the river, not the ground, not the source. Someday you go to the source of the river to find the peace. Do you find the peace there? It's just raining all the time there. [Laughter]

03rd November 2014, 1st Talk
Mumbai, India

Bhakta And *Jñani* Are Two Different Names Of Absolute Non-Ownership

Q: How does Maya play?

K: Maya is the place where you have differences. Two – that's Maya; where there are differences, where you have time and objects of time. All of that is Maya.

Q: And no-time?

K: No time is Maya too. Time and no-time are different, so even that's Maya. Whatever you can make an opposite of, whatever you can name, whatever you can frame, whatever you can imagine – is Maya. But That what you can call Reality is not something you can imagine. You can imagine the name Reality; but by that you cannot imagine Reality. All the rest that you can imagine, that you can either experience or not-experience, it's all maya. You can also call it a dream. Whenever you see your brother, you see maya. [Laughter] When you are sister of somebody, you can be really sure that's maya. Whatever you can imagine as life or existence, especially when you're born, you're really established in maya. So, what to do?

In Mexico, the name 'Maya' means 'I Am', the being. Already 'I Am' is maya.

Q: How to come out of it?

K: The problem is you were never in it! But now, by trying to get out of it, you imagine to be in it. Then you become an imaginary 'I' who needs to get out of something. Then that becomes quite real because whatever you imagine to be is your reality. Now, trying to get out of maya confirms the one who wants to get out. Whatever you do now is against being what-you-are. Expecting that by doing or not-doing you would get out of maya, puts you into the dream.

Then I sit here and say, what to do? There's nothing you can do or not do to get out of Maya because the problem is there was no one in Maya in the first place. You imagine yourself to be born, you imagine yourself to be a person. Even to imagine to be God is an imagination. What to do? Even God imagining to be God is Maya! This is the last dimension you die in. Now you try whatever you try to get out of it. It will not work. So, what to do?

Whatever you do or don't do is in Maya; it has to stay in Maya. Whatever you enter, wherever you find yourself, is Maya. By not finding yourself at all, maybe you're something that could not be found. That way, the only way out of the idea that you can be something that could be experienced or is an experience.

Maharaj's ultimate medicine is not finding yourself: looking everywhere but not finding yourself anywhere. Now you believe that you found yourself, as someone who's born as a body. That's misery, you know that – a permanent existential crisis! It's natural to long to get out of it. But whatever you do from that position confirms you. It's quite a perfect trap. As more you want to get out of the prison, you remain a prisoner: totally perfect trap made by yourself. Fantastic!

You cannot even blame anyone else, not your parents, not your brother. Maybe you can blame your brother. [Laughter] It doesn't work but it's always fun in the family to blame someone. Because you are, I Am!

No. If you ask me what you should I do, I say just have another coffee because you cannot do anything anyway. But at least enjoy yourself, because whatever comes next will not give you a solution to your problem which no one has.

Q [Another visitor]: Am I in Maya between birth and death?

K: No. You were before not born, with this body you are not born, and after this body That what is-not born. In birth no one is born. So, no one is in Maya. Now you are not born, you are still that what-you-are prior to birth and will be after death. You're prior to birth, beyond death and now what-you-are.

Q: That is the actual position...

K: That is your Absolute position.

Q: But now I consider myself to be this body...

K: That's the phantom that considers himself to be born. The Self will never consider anything. Your nature never considers anything. The phantom considers to be born.

Q: So, is it the phantom that considers that it will die?

K: What else? A dead phantom sees his future, being dead.

Q: But prior to birth there was no phantom...

K: Maybe even now there is no phantom because you cannot find the substance of it; you cannot even say it exists. You just have an experience of something which is an idea, but you cannot even say if it exists or not. If you really look into it, it's already gone. So, it even doesn't exist now. It's just that a concept appeared but it's not even there now. There is no birth in birth and no death in death because the phantom never existed. It's a dream object, it's a dream imagination. So, what is there now?

The only Reality which was, is and will be is That what-you-are. Life now living itself in an idea of an imaginary 'I' is still Life.

So, only Life is real now. Life was, is and will be a Reality – the Absolute Life. Now experiencing itself in a dream-like body or anything doesn't make life less Absolute. Only Life is Reality and whatever you realize now, is what? A dream-like living.

Life is never born and never dies and the life you can experience now is already gone – never happened.

Q: And yet all of us are here?

K: All this is shadows of life.

Q: Do they all experience...

K: No, they're all experienced by Life. No shadow can experience anything: all the shadows of this whole universe is experienced by life. But there's no experiencer here which is real. The only Absolute experiencer is Life itself. So, you are experienced by Life, [Pointing to himself] this is experienced by Life and all of this [Pointing to visitors] is experienced by Life – lived by Life. Life is living all of that, but only Life is real and not the way it lives itself.

There are no experiences here that are real. There are just points of views of Existence looking at itself – reference points. It's like cameras sitting here. But That what perceives, the Absolute Perceiver, is not different here or there. It's just different ways of perception. The question always is, who perceives the perceiver?

So, what is the Absolute Seer? That you can call Life or Existence. The Absolute Seer experiencing itself in all relative seers or shadows. So, nothing happens here; it's just Absolute existence experiencing itself in relative ways. But experiencing itself in relative ways doesn't make it relative. It's always Absolute. It was, is and will be the Absolute and that is your very nature. That's the nature of everything. Whatever is, the nature of it is Life itself. Life itself is the only Reality and the realization of it is not different. Life cannot find Life in its own realization. Reality cannot be found anywhere, because if it could find itself, there would be two realities. That's an idea, that's an imagination. No second Reality – that's

Advaita! Absolute *Parabrahman* experiencing itself as Brahman. So, nothing happened!

Q: Why do all the shadows...

K: Shadows experiencing to be real... they're real shadows.

Q: All the shadows experience the waking state and the dream?

K: No. Existence experiences the waking up of someone who wakes up. If That which wakes up is there before waking up, there is no waking up in waking up. There is no awakening in awakening, no birth in birth, and no death in death. That's the nature of life. In birth no one is born, in waking up no one wakes up, because the nature of one who wakes up is already absolutely there – totally awake – never sleeps, never is awake! It just exists Absolutely before the experience of waking up happens. So, nothing ever happens. It's all bad for the doer because he cannot do anything. Whatever he does, whatever he achieves, whatever he understands is... [Blowing in the wind]

I know it's tricky when you see all the masters and the seven billion unique shadows; everyone has different parents, different conditioning and all those differences. Every day is different, every moment is different. And then the Self is supposed to be That what never changes. [Laughing] What to do? It is not by understanding that something happens.

Q [Another visitor]: An organized question...

K: [Laughing] The organizer who wakes up in the morning always has a question. How can I make life nicer, says the orga-nicer. This organ wants to be nicer says the organizer.

Q: Can you say something about the law of cause and effect?

K: There is no cause and no effect in Reality.

Q: Doesn't look like it...

K: You call it Maya because only in maya there's cause and there's effect. There are differences and then you make the cause different from the effect. That's Maya, when something comes from something, then you make it Maya. Creator creating something that's not the creator, that's maya, that's cause and effect. This moment is cause of the next moment or you are the cause of this question. That's maya, it's an illusion.

Q: It doesn't feel like it...

K: That there's a questioner with questions with a German life, the cause of it is because you believe to be born. The cause of all your problems is the root thought 'I' who believes to exist. Even before birth, the root thought 'I' believes to exist and then comes the questioner – I am what? Then he wants to be nice, he has a preference. The preference from the beginning is not to exist. It's always a 'Why'. Why do I have to exist?

And I sit here and say, Why not? Does it make you more or less? That one now who is in dream of more or less, than you are in the maya that something is nice and something is not so nice. You want to get out of the discomfort of existence.

Q [Another visitor]: Is there something that decides the comfort level of someone?

K: It's all discomfort. The moment you're a person, you're in a discomfort. You're a doubtful existence.

Q: That's fine...

K: That's not fine. If that really would be fine, you would not sit here. Nothing is fine enough. The moment there's a definer, he wants to be finer. He wants to have the fine, not this gross body here. At least I want to be the spirit and not this bloody body. Then he wants to be awareness because awareness is better than this one. Because awareness is superior, awareness is the finest you can get. So, you get established in awareness because that's the finest. But for all of that, there has to be one who defines and makes differences of good and bad – this is not so fine and that's fine. All of that is maya.

Whatever tells you that your true nature is awareness and this is not what-you-are, again makes a difference. By realizing yourself as awareness, you already make it as your finer place. This presence as a person is bad, so you think the presence as awareness would be good. So, there's an advantage of awareness. But the question is who needs it? Maybe even awareness is part of maya.

Does Absolute life need any special circumstance or any special way of living itself? Does Life need to be aware to be life? Is awareness of life better than unawareness of life? Or do you need to be aware that you don't even need to be aware?

Q [Another visitor]: So, is language a tool to get out of maya?

K: You believe! When we now talk about awareness, you need words, but awareness doesn't need any word to be awareness. The Bible says in the beginning there was the word 'I' and it was good. When God wakes up, what does he say? God! Then he starts realizing itself. Then he becomes Brahman. There's nothing wrong in it. Now that you forgot that in coming nothing came and there's no other God – that's maya. Believing that you would have a better place somewhere, that you have to do something, that you lost something.

Q: I believe that with language I can get out of maya...

K: Try harder! By language you cannot come out of where you were never in.

Q: So, how did you do it?

K: I never did anything. I never realized myself. Did I ever claim that I realized myself? It's a very important thing. I tell you I never realized my true self. There would never be anyone who realizes his true self – not even the Self. And I'm absolutely happy that I can never and don't need to realize myself to be what I Am. There's no need of realization for me to be what I Am.

Q: So, it just happened?

K: It never happened. For what I Am and what-you-are, nothing ever happened. Then how can language get you out of that where nothing ever happened? Language is part of happenings.

Q: The first 'I' thought occurs when you are three years older...

K: Then you start identifying yourself with the body. This becomes a home and then language becomes the tool of this home. Then you're fucked. Having a food body and taking care about it. Then you're always thinking how to get out of this business. I don't want to be a caretaker of this piece of – whatever.

Q: And for you it was the same?

K: Why not?

Q: And was there a moment it stopped?

K: I still care about this body. Why should I not care about this body? I drink, I eat, I go to toilet, I take showers. [Laughter] I just take care, or it takes care of itself – call it whatever. But you may say that there was never any one and now there's no one who takes care whether it takes care or not. That what I Am never cared whether this one takes care or not. With the body comes the caretaker, every morning it wakes up together with the body. It's like co-existence. An accident happened, then there is a caretaker and there's something to take care about. That happens every morning by waking up.

But prior to that, in spite of the presence or absence of this caretaker and the object that he takes care about is That what is your nature. Life is uninterrupted. It now experiences itself as a caretaker, taking care, but it doesn't make Life a caretaker, so it doesn't have to stop. So, there's no way out, but no need to get out. This is your realization, what can you do? Because you are, this shadow is. There is a shadow that wakes up with the shadow body.

I never claimed that now I have an advantage – absolutely not. I'm absolutely happy that I don't need one. And I never got out of anything because if I could get out of anything, I could get out of what I am. Then there would be two, me and something else. This is what I am. This is I Am That – whatever it is. How can I leave what I am by any language? Did that work for anyone?

Q: I don't know...

K: But you thought that I got out by language. Any other good ideas? [Laughter]

Q [Another visitor]: A king who dreams to be a beggar, how does he wake up to become a king?

K: King that wakes up seeing a king makes him a beggar. The moment you have an image, even if you're the king controlling the whole universe, you're still a beggar compared to That what is the universe. That what is God, what is life, can never get more or less as it is. By that it owns whatever can be owned. But a king needs a kingdom, so he's a beggar. He owns nothing. He is an imaginary king of an imaginary kingdom. He just has to look into a mirror to see a beggar.

The same is with knowledge: the one who knows the whole universe, all the secrets of the universe, all what can be known, is still an ignorant idiot compared to the Absolute Knowledge that never needs to know anything to be what-it-is. The biggest pandit, the biggest scholar is just an absolute idiot. It's all relative knowledge. You can know the relative knowledge of the entire universe, but you cannot know yourself. The same is with the king. He can have the biggest kingdom of all times, but he still is a beggar.

But instantly when you are what-you-are, you are the owner of what is and is not. Being the Absolute owner of life by being Life, there is nothing to beg. But a king is begging for a kingdom to do what I want: if one doesn't do what he wants, he cries. So, what about the kings, the dictators, the Avatars and the gods? They are merely dream objects of what-you-are. They cannot deliver anything for you. They're just beggars – even the biggest gods you can imagine. Compared to what-you-are, they're beggars.

I always make a joke that the President of America, the most powerful human on earth compared to a beggar on street in India, there is more personality in the beggar then the President of America. The beggar on the street knows his place and has an acceptance, but the President of America, four years or eight years, then he's gone. So, it's very fragile. He has to do whatever he has to do to get elected again. So, he is a beggar for acceptance of people. But the beggar is just a beggar – give me something or not, fuck you anyway. In that sense a beggar is more in peace as he knows his place.

I'm a beggar here always begging for questions, [Laughter] and you are like a king who allows me to answer. I'm just a tool for your inexhaustible curiosity.

Q [Another visitor]: We are all beggars seeking ourselves...

K: Yeah. You're begging for knowledge. Knowledge begging for Knowledge, isn't it fantastic? Self begging for Self, Peace begging for Peace. You can go on and on and on. It's quite a joke. The Absolute existence begging for whatever. Isn't it fun?

Q: I'm miserable...

K: You're begging for being miserable? When you beg for something believing that you need something, that makes you a beggar. Then it's miserable. It makes you a 'me' who is in me-sery of not having enough – instantly. If you pray to God, you become a beggar. If you pray to God and you want something more, you become a beggar. You make yourself depending on a mercy of a higher whatever: that makes you a beggar. Then you make your well-being, your happiness, depending on someone giving you something. That's misery! Any happiness that depends on a special circumstance of getting something or fulfillment of an outside event makes you a beggar depending on the fulfillment.

That what is Satisfaction itself, That what is Joy itself, begging for external joy to happen. [Mocking] Mercy on me please, make me happy. Any moment you exist, you are a beggar. Any moment you imagine anything to be, it makes you a beggar. But what to do? Is there something wrong in begging to yourself, asking for something you don't need? You just play: you play the beggar and that what is begging – just for fun. It could happen... maybe it's just a play. You just play as if you need something, you play a beggar. In nature you do it anyway.

You act as a beggar but what-you-are is not a beggar by acting like a beggar. Maybe acting like a 'me' is like an actor playing his role. But maybe now you forgot that you're just playing a role. It's just a role you play but it's not your nature. Maybe you're the Absolute actor playing all the roles but you're none of the roles that you play, you're Absolute actor who plays all the roles. But as Self you can never play your own role. Whenever you act to play a role, you play a role of whatever you can imagine. Its acting and you always get an Oscar for that. The best actor award. There's no other actor, that's the problem. You will bag the Oscar anyway. You are the one and only. [Laughter]

Q: But there's no real reward in being this actor...

K: It doesn't matter. You play as if you need it. Otherwise why would you go for it? You play hungry, even if you're not hungry, you play to be hungry. But now you forgot that it's just a play and I just sit here to remind you – come on, it's just a play! You only play being earnest, being sincere. But you play it very well. You even believe yourself, that's the whole problem. You play your role so perfectly, that you believe yourself to be that. You're so convincing, you are the Absolute actor. Now you forget to be an actor because you believe in whatever you play.

It's like Shiva having a puppet house full of puppets. Then after a while he forgets that he's playing with puppets and himself becomes a puppet. Now I have to sit here and remind Shiva – come on it's just a play! Nothing ever happened to you! You never got less by playing and you will never become more when you don't play. Your nature is the quality of Life and not the quantity depending on some more or less coming out of something. Your nature was never hungry. But now you play as if someone who is hungry for himself.

Now trying as a seeker to get out of the play is part of the play. It doesn't mean you get out of the play. The absolutely best seeker ever will never find what he's looking for. Maybe the whole problem is you never lost yourself, how can you find it? But you do 'as if'. All these pointers. Do they work? Does language work? [Laughter]

Because you want to have wisdom by learning, you are wisdoomed. This idea that you can get wisdom by learning, you're doomed by that. You're doomed by trying to become wisdom. Every moment you try to become yourself, it's a doomsday. You're doomed to be a seeker. And it will never end because you'll never find yourself. Doomed means there's no end to it. Doomed for eternity to look for yourself! That's called consciousness. It will never stop inquiring into its nature. Consciousness is totally doomed to look for itself. Then you expect from consciousness to give you the answer. Even Consciousness is doomed to inquire into its nature infinitely. Doomed for eternity to inquire into its nature, that's called consciousness. The lover, the loving and the beloved – Consciousness – in an infinite affair with itself, never ending.

And I sit here and tell you that you better be in spite of consciousness looking or not looking or inquiring. If you ask me, it will never stop inquiring. Out of love, it would always want to know what-it-is. The moment consciousness is, there's a lover and then the lover wants to know the beloved – himself. It will never stop. Because there are no two consciousnesses, it can never know itself. So, there will never be an end to it. But the love for itself will never stop. Out of love for itself, it will look into its nature, in whatever way. Never-ending story! That's why we're sitting here.

Q: Is it love or obsession?

K: What is the difference? You are obsessed because you love; you have a passion for yourself because you love yourself. So, you're obsessed by that. It's like the passion of Christ, comes out of the love of God, wanting to know God. The reason of all this is love; and you are possessed by that idea. Now we are trying to make an exorcism here – from an occupied soul with an idea. Does it work? The devilish idea that you can know yourself? This demon that came over you, the demon ego.

How can you destroy this demon? How can you exorcise it? How can you get rid of that demon you believe to be – the ego. Any idea?

Q: Don't believe in that idea...

K: Does that work? When you ignore it, you confirm that there is one. That's the whole problem. If you want to kill him, you confirm that there is one. Try harder. You cry about him, that doesn't work either. Do you think when you cry so much the demon would not be able to take it? How to kill that phantom ego?

Q: Does it ever rest anytime?

K: Why should it rest? It's inexhaustible. It doesn't need to rest. The moment you wake up, it's there waiting for you, full of energy. It's a reflection of you. As Absolute energy you are, so is this demon. It's like a reflection of yourself in a mirror; the ego. The phantom is as real as you are. Then you want to kill it, you want to exhaust it, you want to ignore it. All those techniques – I meditated away, I don't see it anymore, I ignore it. [Chanting] Om... When I wake up and open my eyes, the ego will be gone. Ego – go. Demon, leave me. [Laughter] I dug the grave for the demon and the phantom will now be in grave and now I close the grave. When I open my eyes, I will be free of the ego. [Laughter] I have fun everywhere I see meditators. I see undertakers and diggers.

You try to close your eyes like an Ostrich burying his head in the sand thinking that when I am not, the ego is not. When I comeback from my deepest self, the ego must be gone because you think when I'm gone so long, the ego cannot wait so long for me. [Laughter] I go to the deepest of the deepest soul of my inner direction. I go to the void, where even I am not and when I come back I would've burnt it out by my absence. [Laughter]

Everyone reads the books of people who made it and had an experience of whatever kind and since then, no 'me'. There's a guru in America called Swami No Me. Many me's like one with no 'me'. Is no 'me' still one 'me' too many? What would you say? Is the 'me' which is not there still there or not? Who is this 'me' who is not there anymore? Is the absence of 'me' still too much 'me'? The question is always who needs the absence of 'me' to be what one is? What 'me' needs the absence of the 'me'? And who recognizes that there is no 'me'? I always have these questions. Who experiences the presence of the 'me' and who experiences the absence of the 'me'? Me? [Laughter] Then who tells the others that he has no 'me'? [Laughter] What 'no me' tells another 'me' that here is no 'me' and gives himself the name 'no me'? Toilet is everywhere, outside and inside. You go out and then you go into a toilet and come out of toilet without shit. [Laughter] But you cannot get rid of the shitter, the shitter is still there. The cheater who will cheat himself again and again. The shitter without a shit has a potential shit.

Q: Waiting to be released...

K: You want to get rid of the shit and then you want to fast as long as you can. Then you say I'm fasting because I don't want to have something to digest. I got rid of my personality and now I make sure that I get established that I don't take anything anymore. I'm totally in *vipasanna*, there is no story anymore, there is no before and no after, I have to be just quiet, nothing happens, I have no family, no friends, no story, I never woke up, I don't go to bed. [Laughter] It's quite a hard work! Not to make a story anymore, you really have to work your ass off. [Laughter]

Q: Even then there's a story...

K: The no-story is a bigger story because the ownership still runs. Now I'm the owner of no-story. I have no-story, I'm never born. Ha, ha, ha... Who is never born? It's all blah, blah, blah. It's all a language blah, blah, blah, it means nothing. It's just a statement coming out of someone – I have no story. It's like if you say I am God, it means nothing. You can repeat it for thousands of years, it has no impact. I am the Self – so what? No time or no shit is still full of shit. It makes it even worse; the shit you don't see stinks even more.

Q: You said when you see a woman you see an animal...

K: Even when I see a man, I see an animal. [Laughter] I only see animals. Anima in Greek means soul. Whenever I see anyone, I only see anima, the beast, the consciousness. That consciousness has some figure. What makes woman a woman?

Q: [Laughing] The same thing that makes man a man...

K: Woman would say emotions, intuition. Women tell me that only women have emotions and intuitions and men can never get that. There are so many concepts of what makes a woman, what is a woman and what is not. In the Absolute sense, the male and the female principle, the life and the living. It's not like having breasts makes someone female. When Buddha says the woman principle will never get enlightened, even the male principle never gets enlightened. Even Life will never know itself as the living never knows itself. But everyone takes it like a gender.

Even Jesus said that you can only go to the father through me by that he means that you have to go through the awareness to the father. But is that true? Or does it still confirm the one who has to go through something? I have no idea. Does any religion needs any ideas that something has to be done? As Jesus he was really like a messenger, a messiah. But as Christ he destroyed everything. He said no one will ever enter the kingdom of heaven – no one. So what to do? Does that mean there is a before and after?

Q [Another visitor]: You said that Christ was initiated in the fourth state but Jesus was not?

K: Yes. Jesus became Christ, the initiated one – Christus. They changed his name.

Q: When he was resurrected?

K: Jesus died on the cross but the nature of Jesus which is Life could not be killed on the cross. It went to the absence of life – the dead. But life cannot be killed by the absence of life. From there on, Life was resurrected as Christ. Then going into the blue again, as does everything.

Q: But even that is too late?

K: It's a story that repeats itself all the time. It's an infinite story of one who starts as a person and then goes to the end of awareness. Then by accident gets initiated like Ramana experienced that he cannot be killed by anything, that death cannot touch him. Then coming back as the immortal nectar, that your life cannot depend on presence of any experience. That what is your nature is never depending on any life experience, that you now call life or body or anything. It's always the same in all traditions.

Q: So, Ramana was in the fourth state when he got that?

K: He was not in the fourth state. That what is Ramana experienced the absence of life and the veil dropped. The idea, the maya that life is depending on an experience of life to be Life, that dropped! But that doesn't make Ramana going to the fourth state. No one is in the fourth state. Life is now blinded by the idea that it needs to be alive. Like in your case, you believe that you need a body that you're born, that something will happen, that you can die. But if you experience absolutely That what-you-are, that you are Absolute without this person you believe to be, then this person never existed. Then what-you-are which is without that person, without the universe, without any experience, that's Reality. It was there before, but there was a belief that it needs something. The belief system drops. Then you're initiated in that state in which there is no 'one' who is initiated. It's just like Life without dreaming.

Q: But that's not what Reality is...

K: That is Reality that never needs to realize itself to be Itself. What else is Reality? Reality not knowing itself and never needs to know itself to be Reality – that's Reality! That's the fourth state, that's

Samadhi. Your nature, your natural state without any experience of anything. No need of anything – that's *sat-chit-ananda*. That's the fourth state.

Q: But you said the fourth state is not the Reality...

K: It's not a state, its what-you-are. There's no state, it's just for the sake of language you mention it that way. These are the scholars; they want to nail you down. They are the nail makers and the hammers. [Laughter] They want to make it a state. It is not any state.

Q: First, second and third are states...

K: And fifth, sixth and seventh as well. [Laughter]

Q: Except the fourth? [Laughter]

K: There are relative states and there are Absolute states. The Absolute states don't have any state. So, there's a state but there's no state. There's home but there's no home. That's your natural state – nature not knowing any nature at all and doesn't need to be nature because there's no idea of nature left. No image of anything and still you are.

Q: I want to remove the paradox...

K: How can you remove the paradox? You are the paradox. You want to make it as something that can be known and by that you'll suffer, I tell you. You're greedy to know yourself and you want to make something what is an object of knowledge and by that you'll suffer. You'll always miss it because whatever you try to understand now is a misunderstanding.

Q: I understand that there's no use of understanding what I am... [Laughter]

K: Even that is a misunderstanding. [Laughter] Especially the one who says that I don't try to understand that I don't need to understand. In that way, all one can say is bullshit.

Q: I was just pointing out that Reality is neither state nor no-state...

K: I said there's neither state nor no-state, there's just Life as that potential without any dream of life. That would never make itself a state. Now when talking, we make it something. We call it Reality but Reality will never call itself Reality. *Parabrahman* will never call itself *Parabrahman*. Now in this maya we call it *Parabrahman* or *Paramatma* but *atma* will never call itself *atma*.

Q: Is *atma* the 'I Amness'?

K: *Paramatma* is that *atma* that doesn't know any *atma*. When atma knows *atma*, there're two *atma's* too many. [Laughter] When someone says I know, then for sure there's one knower too many. Like the Arc of Noah, he wants to survive.

Q: *Atma* is like a soul?

K: The Absolute soul of God, that's *Paramatma* – that's the nature of soul – who doesn't have any soul. And That what is soul has no soul. It would never call itself soul.

It's an old tradition. Even the Blavatsky Theosophical Society has the seven states. We are talking about the seven states and here everyone wants to get out of the first and the second state. People always complain that first we should go through the first state and not directly go to the what-you-are, that's not possible. First you have to go through the three states for many lifetimes before you may be accidentally slip into the fourth state. Can you wait so long? There must be a short-cut.

No. All there is are detours. Even the short-cuts are detours. Anyway, even the shortest one, is too long.

Q [Another visitor]: In a short-cut there is no waiting...

K: But you wait for the language to deliver you something. [Laughter]

Q: How is it possible to have a short-cut?

K: It is a dead end because whatever has a short-cut or a detour will die. Whatever claims to have a short-cut to the end, is a dead end. It means dead ends. Where dead ends, life starts!

Q: Sounds fantastic...

K: So, go for it. It's all too long. This is a dead end here. Whatever is born has a dead end.

Q [Another visitor]: When Awareness is, the phantom is not?

K: Even in awareness there's a phantom because you make awareness as an object.

Q: If it is made as an object...

K: The moment you talk about it, you make it an object. The moment you make awareness different from consciousness or whatever, you make it an object.

Q: Now when we are talking about it, we are aware that there's no awareness...

K: But when you are not aware, you will never talk about awareness.

Q: We will not talk because we are aware...

K: Who is aware?

Q: Awareness is...

K: Who says that awareness is?

Q: Now when I'm talking I talk about awareness. But when I'm not talking, I'm just aware...

K: So, when you're not talking you're more aware?

Q: Awareness is when I just see this fan...

K: Who sees this fan? What awareness sees this fan?

Q: Awareness comes first, then comes the phantom...

K: Maybe whatever comes first is already a phantom.

Q: I just heard your words...

K: No you don't hear my words because there's one who wants to understand. When there's listening, there's no listener. When there's one who hears and wants to understand, that's trying and not listening.

Q: When I'm really listening...

K: When there's really no you really listening, how can there be one who is not listening?

Q: If listening happens...

K: Listening is not a happening. Perception is not a happening. Perception never happens.

Q: Then what happens?

K: I don't know. Whatever you claim happens, but not perception. The perceiver happens but not perception.

Q: Perceiver happens after the perception happens...

K: Perception never happens. Perception is perception with and without perceiving anything. That's why it's called the eye of God, with and without perceiver there's perception. Perception is never-never. That's the eye of God which is never closed or open. The Absolute seer is the Absolute seer, that's the Absolute perception. Then there's a perceiver or no-perceiver. When there's no-perceiver there's nothing to perceive, that's absence. With a perceiver there's perceiving of what can be perceived, that's presence. Perception is experiencing itself in the presence and absence – with and without perceiver. But perception is uninterrupted.

Q: So, there's a perception with or without perceiver...

K: But perception is never a happening.

Q: You said perception can be with or without perceiver...

K: It cannot 'be'... It is that what is Life living itself and Life is never-never, Life is perception: It's the eye of God, the Absolute Seer. In seeing and not-seeing, it is. In not seeing there is no seer and in seeing there's a seer. So, what is real? The difference or That what is never different in the difference? That what is never happening is That what is Reality. The happening of a seer and the happening of a non-seer are both maya and a happening of realization, but not Reality. And perception is not a happening. There has to be perception so that a perceiver can appear. That a perceiver can be perceived, perception has to be there before the perceiver is. So, the perception is with and without the perceiver or presence of anyone or anything.

Q: I'm saying the same thing...

K: You said perception is a happening. It's not. When you say that perception is happening, there needs to be a perceiver for which perception is happening. When there's perception, in that the perceiver is a happening. You can say the perception is the fourth state which is uninterrupted. You make that as a happening which is not a happening. It's like an understanding which is not an understanding. It's like a knowledge which is not a knowing. But you make it a knowing, that which is not a knowing.

Q [Another visitor]: When Krishnamurti says the observer is the observed, what does he mean?

K: Ask him. I never read him; I was never interested in him – too complicated. I'm much too lazy to read it. I was tired even before I started reading. [Laughter] Always by intuition I knew that it cannot be so complicated. It must be very simple. It has to be like knowing yourself as you know yourself in deep-deep sleep where there is no one who is or is not asleep. That's the knowledge you are which is independent of any presence or absence of anything. That's all. And the rest, no one needs to know. That's a direct pointer to what-you-are which never needs anything to be what-it-is. The rest is like a mind-fuck. Absolute, infinite, mind-fuck. Very intelligent mind-fuck, but mind-fuck nonetheless.

It has to be a direct experience that what-you-are is prior to that experiencer. If the experiencer is real, it should be uninterrupted.

But it's not. But That what is experiencing the experiencer is uninterrupted – it was, it is and it will be. Finished! And establish yourself in that which is never coming in coming and not going by going. Be that – finished! Be what-you-cannot-not-be – finished! And not observe the observer, be the witness, blah, blah, blah... As I said, I'm already exhausted trying to understand what he means by that.

The simplicity of being what-you-cannot-not-be which is in spite of presence or absence of any kind – which never needs anything. No one complains about the deep-deep sleep. That is called joy, that is called peace, that is independent of any presence or absence of understanding or one who understands or puts it into a language or not, having a higher or lower tra... la... la...

That's called your natural state, which is Samadhi. You may call it the fourth state, but you don't have to call it anything. Just be that what-you-cannot-not-be which is with and without whatever you can imagine. Never demanding any difference of presence to be what-it-is.

That what you were when you were born, this presence which has never experienced itself as Presence. That what is the Presence of presence where even the experience of presence is second hand because what-you-are doesn't need any presence to be what-it-is. You are in absence as you are in the presence, what-you-are. That is what-you-cannot-not-be. The rest is [Blowing] just a fart in the wind of that what is called consciousness. Consciousness needs to know all that, it is interested in all of that because consciousness already is ignorance and ignorance wants to know itself. Consciousness is dependent on being conscious. It needs to be conscious: there has to be consciousness.

All there is, is consciousness, I agree. But what-you-are is in spite of all of that what-it-is, not because of it. So what?

Q: And that can never be realized?

K: That is ever-realized, it never needs more realization, it is Reality!

What is more realization than Reality? And the rest is what? They are real-lies. Who needs to know what-it-is? Only the one who is in the dream needs to know the dream, what-you-are never needs anything. That's why it is itself Absolute Satisfaction. And none of this circus of understanding, of the clowns, who claim they have no 'me', can give it to you, the 'me' clowns and the 'no me' clowns. Do you want to be an acrobat of words?

Q: For myself as long as the 'me' is there, being bhakta is fine enough...

K: When there's *bhakta*, there's no 'me'. What would you say what is a *bhakta*? Do you think *bhakta* and *jñani* in nature are different? They are two different names of Absolute non-ownership. Both don't own anything. So, *bhakta* has given up *bhakti* and jñani has given up *jñana*. So, they don't even know if they are *jñani* or bhakti or anything. There's no idea anymore of what they are and what they are not. The Self gave up the Self by being what-it-is. But how can that be done? It's not a doing.

Just by being what is the Self without knowing any Self. That's the way it is – by being what-you-cannot-not-be. That makes you a *bhakta* which is Self, which is the Absolute. That is 24 by 7, it's never-never. But it's not an action, it's not a happening – never was, never will be. Not because of you doing anything or not doing anything. You are That. So, you cannot claim that you have done something or something happened. It's Absolute in spite and never because, of whatever you can imagine you are.

Q [Another visitor]: When I say, 'Who Am I?' there's still an entity that's still asking the question...

K: Then it's not a right inquiry. Who Am I is a technique which is not pronounced. 'Who' means the world, Am means the spirit and I means the Awareness. First Who [Opening the thumb index finger and the middle finger], then Am [Closing the middle finger], then I [Closing the index finger] and then you [Closing the thumb] start. You are the answer to that question. It's not like one who questions in the beginning 'Who Am I' and then someone waiting for an answer somewhere. No. You are the answer to that question, Who Am I. What you are, is the answer to the question Who Am I – silence. There's no answer in it, but you are the answer. There's no answer like I Am the Self or God or anything. There's just That what-you-are who doesn't know Itself at all. There's knowledge of existence.

'Who' [Opening thumb, index finger and the middle finger] is the world. 'Am' [Closing the middle finger] is the spirit and 'I' [Closing the index finger] is awareness. But when awareness ends, you start [Closing the thumb]. You are the answer to that question Who Am I. You are prior and beyond I.

Q: Then who asks this question?

K: There is no questioner. The world is questionable, the spirit is questionable and the awareness is questionable. So, 'Who' is the question, 'Am' is the question and 'I' is the question. In spite of the question 'Who', in spite of the question 'Am', in spite of the question 'I', you are. You are the Absolute answer to all what you can question. The universe you can question, the spirit you can question, the I you can question. But the I of the I, the answer, the Silence, the Absolute presence of what-you-are, there is no doubt anymore. So, doubt [Opening thumb, index finger and the middle finger], doubt [Closing the middle finger], doubt [Closing the index finger] and doubtlessness [Closing the thumb] Who Am I is the question to that doubtlessness you are. You are the answer to all your questions.

It's like meditation. It's not like pronouncing it – Who Am I, Who Am I, Who Am I? No. Who [Opening thumb, index finger and the middle finger], Am [Closing the middle finger], I [Closing the index finger] and [Closing the thumb] That what-you-are. You are the answer! The Absolute answer to all that relative questionable experiences. All of that is only there because you are! But you are not there because that is. You are not because; you are in spite of whatever you can imagine. There's a doubtlessness of Existence. That there is no doubter who can doubt himself. In the world there is one, in the spirit there is one and even in the awareness there is one. But in that [Closing the thumb] there is a satisfaction beyond imagination. That silence alone can satisfy you. There's no longing left. There's no idea of home. There's no idea, no concept at all of existence or non-existence. Only to be that, ends all the seeking and all the longing. Maybe it doesn't even end the seeking and longing. Who gives a shit?

That never cares about anything. There's carelessness there. So, how to go there? Who [Opening thumb, index finger and the middle finger], Am [Closing the middle finger], I [Closing the index finger] and [Closing the thumb]. But there's no one later who says because I pronounced Who Am I, now I am That. It's not like I Am God or I Am Self. No. Silence. That never says anything, never defines itself. It's just what-it-is. There's rest without one who can rest in it. That rest what never needs to rest is the nature of the Absolute rest or peace.

And the rest cannot satisfy you at all. It cannot even satisfy itself. Let it be as it is, so what? You have nothing to get out of that. You cannot get lost in it and you cannot find yourself in it. It is as it is. So, may it be as it is and who gives, what? It doesn't make you more or less as That what is in spite of whatever you can imagine. So, Who Am I is not bad but when out of Who Am I comes one who understood something, it's an understanding again and that is again a misunderstanding. Any understanding is a misunderstanding. Whoever claims now I know my true nature landed somewhere. But wherever you land, you have to depart again.

But that what never came by coming and never goes by going, never departs in anything. There's no transit lounge. In every understanding, there's a transit lounge. You wait for the next plane to come or to go. But because you are That, this is. You cannot stop this and there's no need to stop it even. If it's there or not, who cares? That's 'Who cares!' You just can't get rid of your shadow.

This is your whole shadow. Having or not having a shadow doesn't make you more or less. Consciousness is there because you are but you are not because of consciousness. Consciousness is sometimes there, sometimes not. So what? What to do?

No. It doesn't make you what-you-are because it doesn't give you any answer. That's the beauty of that question. There's no one who understands in that. There's no need to understand in that. All the language dies in that. Everyone wants to look for something, then he runs to find something, then he wants to present it to someone else. Everyone who wants to get enlightened is not for himself, maybe he wants to show it to his friends. [Laughter] Because he wants to shine for the world, a shining example of one who can make it – I made it! You want to be the David Copperfield of enlightenment... I made my 'me' disappear.

The first question is for who do you want to get enlightened? For whom do you want to know yourself? For yourself? Maybe yourself doesn't give a shit if you know or not. Or do you want to know for your friends? For your mother, for your wife? Maybe you just want to escape your marriage. There's always some reason to know yourself. Maybe you have an idea if I am my self, I have no wife anymore. People tell me when you are what-you-are, you don't own anything anymore and you have no relationship with anyone. So, maybe you just want to escape your relationship – with whoever, even with yourself. There are always some reasons, and then you want to have some advantage afterwards.

Q [Another visitor]: Does it really happen? Can there be times when you are without a 'me'?

K: Why not? Everything that can happen will happen. I believe everything. It's all a belief system anyway. Not to believe is hard. It's all a belief anyway. I believe that everything will leave me – that I really believe. And I still will be what I Am. By seeing that everything will leave me anyway and I don't have to believe in it anyway. Believing in it or not, it will be gone one day. So, what to do? Why make an effort to believe what is gone already because one day it will not be there anymore. What to do with it? Shit came, shit will go and you still will be what-you-are. Then there comes another shit.

09th November 2014, 1st Talk
Mumbai, India

On That You Can Rely, That Everything Is A Lie

Q: In Mahabharata, brothers were the worst of the enemies. Why is that?

K: Only the one you love can be your enemy. The one you have no interest in cannot be your enemy. You give a shit if he likes you or not. Only when you love somebody, then he becomes your enemy or friend. The one you don't love doesn't count, he can do whatever he likes, but when you love somebody he can really become your enemy because then you expect something from him. Then if he doesn't fulfill your expectation, you hate him.

If the father doesn't treat you as you like, you hate him for that. That's why it's called a family feud; only in family you can kill. The most killings happen in a family more than any war. In the whole history of mankind, killing happened in families; brother killing brother, father killing son. The most dangerous place on earth is being at home. [Laughter] In the Bible, Cain killed Abel. So, better go out and have fun. Spend some quality time somewhere but not at home. Spend your money outside, forget the family.

Q: Still everyone talks about the family...

K: Because there's money involved – family constipation. How to forgive my father for what he has not done to me? That's the main question. How to forgive your mother for what she never gave you? If you look at your father, you always see yourself. For that you hate yourself. No one wants to become like one's father, me included. But I'm like my father. What shall I do? Having a family is already too much. Being born into a family, having a father, having a mother is already hell.

Maybe you hate that you exist so you blame your parents that you exist. You hate yourself, you hate your parents and then you hate whatever comes with it. Then you want compensation starting with pocket money then heritage – it's never enough. They have to pay for it, that you were born. Then later you say God is guilty that I exist. Now he has to take care. If he doesn't do what I want, then I hate him. Then I worship the devil. God if you don't want me to worship the devil then give me what I want. Everyone is in anger.

Q [Another visitor]: How to behave in society? [Laughter]

K: This is the proof that I'm totally irrelevant. [Laughter] Whatever I've said is all rubbish if this comes out of it. Kill them all, kill whoever you can kill. [Laughter] Get a good machine gun or something. [Laughter] Kill all the neighbors first. Everyone starts around himself then sooner or later there would be no problem of society anymore. [Laughter]

Q [Another visitor]: It's like Kill Bill...

K: Kill Bill is a piece of cake against this. This is what everyone would wish for. Everyone wishes for no neighbors and no one to disturb him. Everyone wants to have his peace – my peace – and they want to know how to get that. That's why he asks how to behave in a society so that society doesn't disturb me. How do I get the best out of society, that's your question?

Q [Another visitor]: I mean so that I can go deeper in my silence...

K: How can I stay deep in my silence so that society doesn't disturb me anymore? You want to get rid of something. I told you get a machine gun so that you can stay in your deep silence. But make it radical, kill everybody. Don't leave anyone alive, not even yourself and then there will be silence. Or you may even start with yourself [Bang], deep silence.

He doesn't want to wake up in his body anymore, he doesn't want to be disturbed because the moment he's in his body, he's disturbed. So, just kill yourself! Just get rid of this piece of disturbance.

Q: No!

K: What no? You asked me, I give you the answer. But he doesn't like the answer, that's all. He wants to have a peaceful solution.

Q: If I disturb someone then I'm disturbing myself even more...

K: Why?

Q: Because that's my nature...

K: Then maybe you go to Himalaya and live alone. The moment you go out of your house, you disturb somebody. You're always not dressed rightly for somebody, you don't move in the right way for somebody, somebody will always find something what's not good with you. You can only disturb and you will only be disturbed by everybody. If you make your peace depending on not being disturbed, it's a relative and fragile one. The peace which is worth to be cannot be disturbed by anything and the peace which can be disturbed is a peace of shit.

That what-you-are doesn't need to prove itself in daily life. There's no daily life for what-you-are, there's no society, there's none of that. For what-you-are, there's only Self. Only for you who claims to be himself, there's now a society and all these ideas. And whatever you try will never be sufficient enough for peace. There will always be disturbance. You can only establish a fragile peace which you call as personal peace. It will always be disturbed sooner or later.

All the forums, all the self-improvement ideas are trying to establish something fragile which can be disturbed again and then you have to go again for another seminar. It's like a money making machine.

Q [Another visitor]: What is the real meaning of crucification?

K: There is a cross, nails and hammer...

Q: That's crucification of the physical body. How to crucify that what you believe to be?

K: Who Am I is the crucification, to fix you on That what-you-are. Every time you ask, you are nailed by that what-you-are – that's crucification. Everything drops away and you're nailed to that what-you-are being That what-you-cannot-not-be and you cannot leave that. There's that what you are which is not coming and not going – totally solid – never born, never dies. That is being crucified to what-you-are.

But if you try to do it yourself, it becomes cruci-fiction. Then it's a fiction that you try to make this body, this person tries to become immortal is cruci-fiction. If grace drops everything, then it's a crucifixion. Normally a seeker tries to nail himself but it's only with rubber nails. He wants to hang on, he wants to survive in that. He wants to have an advantage from it, he wants to have a personal peace. He wants to be fixed because he wants to be quiet. If I'm quiet, then I'm in peace. Then maybe the world is in peace. There's an expectation in it. In meditation you try to go to a place where there's silence and you can be in that silence. That's fiction. [Pointing to a visitor] Like he tries to become a silent person, that's fiction. A person will never be silent enough, no way. And even if there's a peaceful person, it's a temporary fragile peace. Sooner or later there will be a big camel that will step on your toe and you will be disturbed. When you're in peace, even a fly on the wall can disturb you.

The nature of 'me' is disturbing itself, just by existence. Just because it is, it is disturbed. Even to exist is being disturbed. The very root of all the disturbances is 'I', the 'I' who exists. There disturbance already happens. Whatever you do in this world, you fight for peace. There's a little warrior worrying about himself and is disturbed by something. He wants to fix something. Then he starts to meditate on himself. All for fighting that disturbance. He wants to be in peace. He wants to find home where he cannot be disturbed anymore, where he can rest. Everyone fights for resting but fighting for resting keeps you alive. You are a peace fighter, a warrior and Osho was a general in that.

Q [Another visitor]: Why does duality create motivation?

K: Existential fear, that's the ultimate motivation for anything. Any moment you exist, there's a doubt in it, there's a dependency. You have to exist to exist. From that moment on, there's a fear that when I don't exist something may happen that I don't like. So, you fight for your little existence moment by moment. There's an underlying existential fear by you believing that you have to exist. Because of that, you exist already. That's the root thought 'I'. From there comes the rest of caretaker who takes care about himself; trying to survive, trying to do something, fighting for his peace, fighting, fighting, fighting. No end of fighting. Fighting for the land, fighting in family, liberals versus the orthodox. There will never be any end to the fighting. For what? For truth? For peace?

Everyone claims that he fights for peace. But it has to be my way of peace, my peace. It has to be the way I like it.

Q: So, the ultimate motivation is the Absolute motivation?

K: There's no movement in the Absolute. In Absolute there's only silence. You can say the *Parabrahman* dreaming a dream and you can only dream in relative ways. There has to be a dream of good and bad. When there's good and bad, light and darkness, light is fighting against the darkness and darkness against the light. There starts the fighting already. For the moment there's a balance and it seems peaceful. No. The night is eating the day and the day is eating the night. Every morning the day wins and at night the night wins the fighting. If there's some light, there cannot be darkness. If there's darkness, there cannot be light. There's fighting everywhere.

The peace you are as the Absolute realizing itself in war, in polarities. One against the other, good against bad. God against devil, devil against God – instantly. That will never end. That's the Mahabharata in India, fighting will happen. Even before you meet someone, even before you go outside your house, the moment you wake up you fight which thought is better than the other one. Who's now the better one from me? Me, myself and I, who is winning today? What am I doing today? What is going to happen? How do I have to present myself? How do I dress today? Before you are in society, you already prepare for war. The war is already happening, crazy!

So, you better enjoy the war because this is the way you realize yourself. No way out. But it's not a contradiction. Peace realizing itself, the Absolute realizing itself as one in two. When there's two, there's one, there's something happening. Then all these possibilities have to be. As much there's good, there's bad. As much there's fighting, there's peace. As much as there's war, there's some other time. It's always balanced. But there's no moment in this world when there's no fighting. Maybe one half is not fighting but the other half is fighting but you cannot decide which half is yours. Then you want to become a peaceful warrior.

But everyone is fighting for peace. Palestine fighting for peace, Israel fighting for peace – for their own peace. Everyone has a good intention. You cannot find anyone with a bad intention. Everyone fights for family, for peace, for what he thinks is good, for his way of life, my God, my Truth.

So, the moment there's an ownership – 'my' existence – you fight for it. This little mine, so subtle, starts very early. You cannot find where the ownership starts and where it ends. Then there's someone who owns something and he wants to keep it or he wants to destroy it; both are the same. Maybe one day you're fed up with your body and you want to get rid of it and you fight to get rid of it. You still fight. You fight to keep it and then you fight to get rid of it.

Q [Another visitor]: So what to do?

K: Many try to commit suicide then someone comes and saves them. Then there's someone who really wants to survive and gets killed by the next car. The one who wants to live gets killed and the one who wants to die has to live for another fifty years. You never know. Life is really not fair. Maybe everyone who wants to die should die and everyone who wants to live should live. But it will not happen. Life is a bitch, you know that! It always bites you when you least expect it. There's one who always says, why not me? Isn't it fun? Sometimes it's fun, sometimes it's really bad.

No. If you ask me where it starts, it starts when God starts knowing Itself. God out of his Absolute potential starts to know Itself. It becomes conscious to exist. There it all starts. Then there are already two. Then he becomes his own devil because there are two Gods. Then the relative God fights the other one and the opposite.

Q: Then it's just survival...

K: The survival of the phantom God. From that moment, God is an imagination. When he imagines himself, he fights for survival. An imaginary God is a phantom God and the phantom God needs to fight for his existence. Every phantom you meet on the street in the whole world is God believing to exist and then he fights for his existence. That's the way it goes. Then he goes to the seminars, just to have tools for survival and trying to find some better weapons to fight against his fear.

You try to find weapons against your fear or your existence. You think there's one who can give you something which takes away that existential fighting. For that you pay everything. You're ready to pay with your life, just to get rid of that fear. So, what to do? That makes you a seeker and at all costs you want to end that fear. You seek by all means the end of the doubtful existence. And only that what is not doubtful, what is doubtlessness itself can satisfy you. There it ends.

But none of these understandings or weapons you can find can end it. In Tiruvannamalai all these so-called realized persons are fighting who is more realized and in what level. Everyone compares with the other one, who is more or less whatever. His truth and my truth and my truth is deeper than his truth and I'm more Ramana disciple than that one and my Ramana understanding is deeper than your Ramana understanding... blah, blah, blah. Even at that level, fighting, fighting, fighting. Always comparing. What's going on?

Q [Another visitor]: You can never end fear?

K: How can you end life? Life will always realize itself in dream existence. If you believe in your dream existence, you fight for that dream existence.

Q: When there's immense pain, you cannot not fight...

K: You just react to what happens. Sometimes you don't fight when it's meant for you to fight. It's unpredictable. It just does what it does. No. I just sit here and point out don't expect that war will ever end for you. This is a battleground – this relative reality of a person. Don't expect that this war will ever end, between father and son and brother to brother. There's no end to it. Cain and Abel in Bible fighting for more attention from God. Even that you fight for. Cain works like anything and is ignored by God and Abel doesn't do anything but is still loved by God. Then Cain kills Abel because of that reason.

So, maybe it's all about love. You fight for love. You fight for peace. You fight for total attention. You fight for the love that takes you as you are. You want to merge with your beloved. You want to be one with your beloved. And as much you try to become one, you are two. It's an amazing game. The more you want to merge with yourself, you're separate from yourself. It's crazy! You honestly want it and you're earnest and sincere about merging with yourself. But even by that intention, that wanting, you're separated. Then you're in a misery. It's crazy!

Q: It's so tiring...

K: You can never be tired enough. If you really could exhaust yourself, there would be a way out of it. But you'll never be exhausted enough. You're in an inexhaustible love affair with yourself. You cannot stop it. And you love the attention from your beloved, you want the best for you and your beloved and then you fight for it. You want to have peace in that love affair. The more you want to have peace, you fight. It's stupidity. When there are two, when the lover is different from the beloved, there's a fight. You're fighting for you don't even know what, just for love.

Maybe I can make many reasons why it happens. But the main reason is that there are two. That you are existence which is different from another existence. That's unbearable.

Q: Even searching for rest is futile...

K: That's called ceasefire. But you will shoot again, you just need to reload. But all of that cannot touch you. It doesn't make you more or less as you are. So, there's no problem in it. I can make it really dark, but so what? Enjoy yourself because it cannot make you more or less as you are. And you cannot change your dream. This dream will always be like it is. Even God cannot want what he wants. So, what to do? Even Krishna cannot change his creation. Even the Absolute himself has no power to change anything. Isn't it fantastic? As I always say, he has no balls. The Absolute is not a bull in a bullfight with someone. The Absolute is always that what is never in any fight. It's dreaming of separation, it's a duet of what-you-are but there's no two in it. It's an imaginary two in an imaginary fight of whatever.

This experience of war or disturbance, what does it do to you? Nothing. It has never done anything to what-you-are. So, what's the problem in it?

Q [Another visitor]: During his end, even Krishna was looking forward for his death...

K: In Mahabharata Krishna said that even I as the Absolute creator cannot change my creation. You pray to whatever but they cannot help you. No one can help you. They cannot even help themselves. Everything is already fixed. The whole future is already there and you cannot change what is already there. The future demands the next moment to happen. If the future demands you to fight, you will fight. If the future demands that you not fight, by whatever you try, you will not fight. It's already arranged.

Q [Another visitor]: So, even ceasefire will happen only if it's supposed to happen?

K: Maybe that'll never happen. You'll always fire. [Laughter]

Q: The phantom needs some rest to start the firing after some time...

K: Even when the phantom is not firing, he's firing differently. He's always shooting. I agree this is the worst you can ever experience. This being a life on earth, having a body, having a father, mother, family, brother, sister, family, friends. This is the worst scenario you can ever imagine. If you ask me, this is like a hell. Having a body to take care and it will never end. Imagine! This family constellation never ends. And you play all the roles and you cannot not be touched by yourself because every emotion, everything what happens, happens to you. You feel everything by being what-you-are. You feel the feeler, the feeling and what can be felt in the whole totality. What-you-are has no problem with this because there's no impact. It doesn't change anything.

But the moment you are only the feeler who is different from what he feels, then you're in trouble. Then you want to have a good feeling, a wellness feeling, a peaceful feeling.

Q: You say enjoy but it's not easy for the phantom to enjoy this...

K: The phantom never enjoyed anything. The phantom is already enjoyed by that what-you-are. The phantom doesn't need to enjoy anything because there's no need for the phantom to enjoy. The enjoyer is already enjoyed by that what is joy. Even the sufferer is enjoyed by joy. By being joy it can only enjoy itself. Even the experience of the absolute misery of 'me' is enjoyed by what-you-are. And you better be that what is enjoying everything because you are That.

But you fall in love with this miserable 'me'. If this is your reality then every moment to be that is misery. But being what-you-are is joy in that sense. So, you better be that what-you-cannot-not-be because nothing is better than that. Any moment you are not That, you're in misery and you even have to fight for your little misery because the sufferer needs to suffer in order to remain a sufferer. He even fights for suffering. How stupid can it get? What would the sufferer do when there's no suffering anymore? He would create something. Then he suffers that there's nothing to suffer about. Everything is empty, no suffering anymore, what shall I do? He will find a reason to suffer.

You're enjoying the silence by being silence and there's a living movie, a dream in front of you.

Q: What-you-are is enjoying this movie?

K: If you ask me, what-you-are is already enjoying silence. The silence enjoying the silence without any interruption. It doesn't even know the movie. It doesn't even know itself. That silence is uninterrupted. That peace is the only peace which is worth being. And any peace you can find here, you lose it again. For the peace you have here, you have to fight again. So, even having the peace now, you're already fighting for it.

That what-you-are never needs anything – ever. There's no need in anything. It's just enjoying the silence by being That. But this little drama Queen or King in front here will always make a drama out of anything. Even if there's no drama, it will say it is so fucking boring today. What can I do to make it different? It will find a way to make some drama. Why do I always say there will always be problems, don't worry? Even the problem that there's no problem will always be there. So, don't worry about this little problem solver.

It's amazing sometimes in this movie, it's fucking boring. Boredom, boredom, boredom. Then you have to fill that emptiness, you have to fill that void. Then you fight for entertainment, something should happen. Out of boredom, sometimes you go to war. You do whatever to end what some people call as void. Then they say, I'd rather go to war and shoot or get shot. In That what is your nature, there cannot be any boredom because there's no one who could be bored by anything.

Q: But does it need to be entertained?

K: There's no need for entertainment. This is the entertainment of consciousness. This is a play of consciousness. It's like a television. You are always the Absolute perception where all the drama and perceivers and different points of view happen. But the only thing is you cannot change the program. Or you have infinite programs but they are never enough. It's bad but it's not so bad. It's always a paradox. It's very bad and not bad at all.

What did you learn at the forum?

Q [Another visitor]: I learnt to forgive others...

K: And what does that make you?

Q: I understand others better. I don't judge people anymore...

K: That's really bad. Judging is fun. [Laughter] You're spoiling all the fun. What do you want to become? A non-judger?

Q: I don't want to be imprisoned by judgement...

K: But then you're imprisoned by non-judgement. You just change the prison and it can change any moment. Then you're back in business. The circumstance can change and suddenly you feel worse than before. All what you've learnt will not work when the circumstance changes.

Q: Because of the forums I reached here.

K: Fuck the forums! [Laughter]

Q: Without the forums I would not sit here...

K: Without your mother giving birth to your body, you would not sit here. Don't make the forums special. It is not.

Q: I like being here...

K: No one asked me if I like that you are here.

Q [Another visitor]: Do you like the idea of people coming to meet?

K: For me its better if no one comes, then I can go home. [Laughter] You know when I started talking there was an organizer who asked me for two years to sit somewhere and give talks in Berlin. I really resisted for two years. No I don't want to sit in front of some miserable bastards and take money for it. It doesn't help anyway. Then for some nights I could not sleep because of this energy and then I agreed for one weekend. The moment I agreed, the energy was fine, I could sleep. I thought if that helps for me to sleep better, let's try. So, first night four people came and on the second night no one came. I was happy that I don't have to do it – Thank God no one comes. I'm off. If tomorrow no one comes, I will never sit anywhere again and on the next bloody night there were fourteen people. I asked what do you want here? [Laughter]

No one believes me when I say I don't need to sit here and talk. But if it has to happen anyway, I would rather have fun. But not because I need anyone to talk to, I can just watch television. Thank God I have heritage that I don't need the money so much. Thank God to my father that he worked his ass off so that I don't need anything.

Personal progress [Blowing in the wind] What is that anyway? Tell me. You become a better person? Who fucking cares? I like bad persons, at least they're entertaining. Good persons are so fucking boring, they have nothing to offer. I like murderers and killers. You're all murderers because you all murdered yourselves. Imagine I would not like you. You all killed yourself just by believing that you're born. All killers, murderers. Any moment you're not what-you-are, you rape yourself here and now. Rapists, all around here – murderers. [Laughter] I mean it! Rapists who have a progress, progressing in raping yourself. Now I don't rape myself so hard anymore. Fucking rapist!

Forums of self-improvement are forums of murderers, rapists, child-abusers. Every bloody seeker is a paedophile; fucking his inner child moment by moment. He wants to get into his inner child. All these esoteric bastards. [Laughter] Every bloody meditator is a rapist. He wants to rape himself into quietness. Fucking rapists, criminals! All these heart masters, meditation masters are all criminals.

Q [Another visitor]: What is meditation?

K: Crime! [Laughter] It's a crime. The inner child-abuser. [Laughter] You can turn everything around everything. From another reference point you can make whatever looks good as totally bad and the opposite. Fantastic! In Avadhut Gita, Dattatreya said the same, why do you shamelessly meditate? Shame on you. [Laughter] It's a crime against your nature, any moment you meditate and get closer to what-you-are, you make yourself an object of time. That's a crime. As if you could do something to get closer to your nature. Criminals, all the meditating bastards.

All these Germans again wanting to heal the world. Little Hitler's running around the world making forums of fascistic progress of personalities. [Laughter] Fucking fascists! Empowerment of personalities, the powerment of the fighter inside making your inner Hitler stronger. The forum for making your little fascist healthy and strong. [Laughter]

It's nice to make fun about everything. If you spare one thing that should not be made fun about, then you make that one special and sacred. Nothing is sacred, nothing. Just enjoy fucking everything by making fun about it – especially fucking yourself. Who needs this fucking self? And what fucking self needs to be

Absolute? Fucking Absolute that needs to be Absolute. What fucking Absolute is that? [Laughter]

Q [Another visitor]: [Laughing] I picture that you will grow into nice old grumpy man...

K: You have no idea. I will not join your grumpiness. Do you see any feeling involved in what I just said? Any emotions? It's just empty pure fun.

Q [Another visitor]: It's all in the dream anyway...

K: Even if it's not the dream, I have fun.

Q [Another visitor]: Empty of emptiness...

K: I'm fool(full) of foolness or fool of emptiness. [Laughter]

Q [Another visitor]: I like that statement – cultivating stupidity...

K: Only stupidity needs to be cultivated. Only ignorance has progress. Whoever claims that he has made progress, is more stupid than before. A bigger ignorance.

Q [Another visitor]: I read a statement which said if you die with a bank balance; the balance is the time you wasted on earning money...

K: Like he [Pointing to a visitor] meditates for the right balance. In Germany there's a saying that the last shirt has no pockets. So, it doesn't matter how much money you have in bank or not, you waste your time anyway.

Q [Another visitor]: There are many new books coming out. What is the motivation?

K: There's no motivation, it's just a happening out of happiness. No one knows where it comes from. Out of that what is happiness, happening happens. Whatever I try to explain is fishing in the dark. No one will ever know why things happen. The only thing you can say about why is why not? Does it matter if you know why it happens? It absolutely makes no difference. You can make up any story. It will always be good or bad but it will never be the truth because no one will ever know why things happen. And that what is the origin of all happenings doesn't need to know. That what is now fishing in this ocean of concepts, will make up another concept of not knowing anything. Whoever claims that he knows, for sure doesn't know. And That what knows, never says anything. That's the whole problem.

The Silence is always quiet and it knows that what is Knowledge. But that what is now ignorance, will always find another concept of why things happen and what they are and how they are and where do they come from and where do they go to. And all the forums and all the progress is all like a fisherman trying to catch a fish. They will never catch the Self in any ocean because the Self is never in any ocean. Not even in the ocean of life you can catch the fish you are.

Jesus as fisherman failed to catch himself. Then he went into the total absence and then he was the Christ. Now we have to live with the crises of Christianity, another concept came out of that.

Q [Another visitor]: Jesus should've remained a Jew...

K: He is still a Jew. Jesus would never have become a Christian if he would see the Vatican and all what came out of Christianity. I think Christ never would become a Christian. Would you think Buddha would become a Buddhist? Krishna would never be a Hindu.

Q [Another visitor]: Hinduism is a way of civilization... [Laughter]

K: You can call them civil-lies. There are educated lies and uneducated lies. It's all lies. In that sense it's fun to talk because no one knows anything. No one needs to know anything. Fighting about what you don't know is just fun. Religion claims that they have truth. [Laughing] My truth is better than yours, so they must know truth because they have something to fight for. How many religions do we have in India?

Q [Another visitor]: Around three hundred...

K: Three hundred and thirty thousand Gods in India, three hundred religions. There's no shortage of anything here. This is the land of excess.

Q [Another visitor]: I trust that one day it will happen...

K: When will it happen what doesn't happen? What happens now?

Q: Nothing...

K: That's too much. For whom is it nothing?

Q: Nobody...

K: Who is that nobody?

Q: Nobody there...

K: Who says now that there's nobody? When someone shoots in front of you then you better be no one. [Laughter] You don't have to shoot me, I'm already dead. [Laughter] Tricky bastards. Don't waste your bullet on me because I'm already dead.

There is a good joke. UG Krishnamurti was flying to America and there was an American sitting next to him. He asked UG what are you doing for life. UG said I'm retired. 'From what?' asked the American? From retirement, said UG. That was the only way to shut up the American. They're only about money, what are you doing for life, is it worth to know you. [Pointing to a retired visitor] In that way you're totally useless. In Germany they would ask you are you not giving your contribution to the society. [Laughter]

So, how is your profession of retirement?

Q [Another visitor]: Indian men normally retire at sixty. When I was twenty, I decided that I want to retire in forty and then I did business. For last twenty years I'm into this business of trying to know myself...

K: So, do you want to be a spiritual teacher?

Q: I want to first go into Samadhi. I don't know anything how can I teach someone else?

K: First you want to realize before you can tell lies. [Laughter] Basically you don't want to lie to yourself.

Q: Yes...

K: Then you will never speak again. [Laughter] If he really doesn't want to lie to himself, he will never say one word again. You don't even wake up in morning. If you really believe in that you can stop lying to yourself, you will never wake up again. If you really believe that you can stop lying to yourself, you have to die now.

Q: But I'm still trying...

K: Trying will happen forever.

Q: Then what to do?

K: Just lie.

Q: Your philosophy is good to understand but practically...

K: Lie, that's very practical. If you're beyond liars, lie. The moment you wake up, you live your lie. This is a lie, waking up is a lie, beginning is a lie, something to be is a lie, someone to be is a lie, to exist is a lie. Where does the lie start? Where does the *leela* start? Where does this *samsara* start? And in this *samsara* you want to stop lying? [Laughing] In the play of lies you want to stop lying. Is that a play of lie or a play of life? [Laughing] You have made quite a goal in front of you. How many lifetimes would it take to stop lying?

Q: Long, long time...

K: You only want to speak a word when you don't lie anymore.

Q: If I don't know anything, how can I say anything to anybody?

K: You do already. In last days you told me many stories, your philosophy. You said there were three hours of Samadhi. So you already have an idea about Samadhi.

Q: My experience is of no use...

K: Thank God there's no use in any experience. Thank God and praise the Lord – just-in-case there is one – that there is no experience. There's no use of any experience. No one ever needs to experience anything to be what one is. Thank God there's no use of anything. It's all uselessness. The whole dream of whatever is in its nature useless. Nature doesn't need to experience itself to be nature. So, it's all, thank God, useless! This is a dance of useless energy dancing with itself. This is the joy of uselessness.

Imagine life needs to have some use to be real. Something has to be of use, something has to be important, something has to have a deep impact or something has to be whatever. What kind of life would that be? A needy greedy relative life that needs some use. What is that kind of life that needs some use? [Mocking] I need to use you, I need some deep experience. What kind of use is that? For who? The answer is always 'me'. And the 'me' is a lie. The liar needs to lie to himself permanently. Especially that he is looking for truth is the biggest lie. He fears truth more than anything else, this liar. The more he talks about the truth, he keeps the truth away. Especially the one who says 'truthfully', 'honestly'... then the biggest liar appears. An honest liar – the biggest liar ever.

Thank God all is empty and nothing is of any use for anyone. The living words don't need to be used. They don't need to be understood by anyone. They're just there because they're there and not because. There's no cause in it, there's no because. And you don't exist because you understand something. The understanding is because you are and not because you need understanding. You always turn it around. So, what is the use?

Thank God this is all useless. No one needs this guy [Pointing to himself], not even this guy needs this guy [Pointing to himself]. This is a dance of uselessness. These are living words. It's not something that someone can make progress from. It's not as if you listen long enough, you become something. No. This is all a dance of useless empty words. Thank God! Absolute useless!

This is the song of irrelevance. The saying, the hearing, the listening – all is absolutely irrelevant! This is the dance of life which never needs to get anything out of it. No need in anything. No use in anything. No user, no abuser, no abused. All of that is a dance of life not because it needs it. It's just dancing with itself. It's just Shiva's dance with himself. Not because of needing it, just out of joy it's dancing with itself.

Thank God there's no use of anything here especially no use from what I say. Thank God it's all a lie. Whatever can be said is a lie. On that you can rely that everything is a lie. Only on that you can rely. That's the most solid you can rely on that whatever you can say is a lie! Whatever you experience is a lie and it always starts with an experiencer – lie. Only the experiencer has to rely on something. It only needs lie on other lies – lie, lie, lie. That's why it's called the *leela*. The whole manifestation everything is lie-la.

That there are women is a lie, especially for men – who are not there either. [Laughing] Truth is fucking heavy, they all get loaded. They're so truth-full, heavy loaded. But with lies they're singing and dancing. If I tell that for you to become what-you-are, you have to be truthful, you have to be sincere, you have to be honest to yourself, everyone would get heavy – Oh no! I have to be truthful; I have to be earnest with my wife! [Laughter]

Nowadays the idea of enlightenment has become the golden cow. Everyone is dancing around this golden cow of enlightenment with this idea that you can realize yourself. Dancing around the idea of an advantage of a golden cow. Having a goal again and forgetting God in it. If I would not be so lazy, I would cut these ideas of enlightenment.

Okay, that was Sunday night. Whoever has to work tomorrow, just shoot your employer. [Laughter]

09th November 2014, 2nd Talk
Mumbai, India

Meditation Of *Neti-Neti* Means Being The Undecided

Q: What is the essence of the message that you give and what Maharaj gave?

K: The essence is that there is nothing for you to gain here or to lose. Your nature didn't lose itself and cannot gain itself in whatever you imagine. Your Absolute nature was never lost, it was always attained and it cannot get more than it already is. That's the all-time message. The message was always the same from everyone. Different words, different pointers but the message is – You are the very Self, so be it and enjoy yourself. And nothing will make you That as nothing unmade you. It's a dream of forgetting. It's a dream event and by the dream event you did not become what you now believe to be.

Q: How to get out of that belief?

K: No, there is no way out. Every time you try to get out of that belief, you make the belief stronger and more real. Whatever intention you have makes the one who has that intention bigger. Even succeeding in getting rid of that intention makes the sucker bigger. You are born a sucker and you will die a sucker; but you are not the sucker. But a sucker is born and a sucker will die.

The seeker is already there when there is something growing in the mother's womb – a dependent being, always needing something. Maybe in the two liquids meeting, there is already a need and now this is the result of it. Now seeking the higher truth you want to have the universal tit. You want to suck God's tit because the mother's tit is not good enough; always more and more and more.

I always go to Tiruvannamalai in a-titty (sanskrit:atithi) ashram. But it just means a guest house. This is just a guest house and you believe to be a guest in your own guest house. You believe you need to pay to get something. Fantastic! You think you have to clean-up the kitchen; you have to clean-up all the mess you haven't done. At least you try to remove the mess that the former guest has done, of what your parents have done. You take up family constellation.

Q [Another visitor]: Is there any process to know our time of death?

K: Depends on what you want to become. What is your goal?

Q: My goal is to get out of this circle of reincarnation…

K: Because you want to get out of the circle, you are in the circle. One comes with the other. Now you believe to be in the circle, trying to get out of the circle. But by that, you remain in the circle. Trying to get rid of the idea makes the idea. Now you are imprisoned and because you want to get out of the prison, you are the prisoner. What to do? Try harder. What would you be out of the prison? What would you do when you get out of it?

Q: I don't know…

K: But he knows that he is imprisoned and he claims that he doesn't know in what prison. But he knows that he wants to get out and this is not where he wants to be. He thinks he's in a prison but he doesn't even know what the prison is. But he wants to get out of it. He doesn't even know what the wheel of reincarnation is but he wants to stop it.

Q: Of course, I don't know anything. [Laughter] I don't know where I am now…

K: You don't know where you are now and you don't know where to go. If that really would be your true nature, you would be quite happy. If that really would be your knowledge right now, that you don't know where you are and you don't know where you are not – where you come from, where you are and where you go to, you would be quite happy. But your problem is you think you know where you came from. You claim something what you don't know as your reality.

Q: I don't know...

K: It's a fake not knowing because there's an 'I' in front of it. Whenever there is an 'I' in front of it – 'I' know or 'I' don't know – it's a fake knowing and a fake not knowing. It's always 'me' knowing and 'me' not-knowing. A claimer who claims to know and a claimer who claims not to know. A claimer who claims to be something and when he has a little understanding claims to be nothing – 'I am something, I am nothing. I know, I don't know.'

It's all a phantom trying to survive. You know this is not true anymore so you better go to the place of not-knowing because when you don't know, you don't have to defend it. It's a safer place. In the safer place of not-knowing you can remain as a not-knowing phantom. But not here. Here you will be shot; knowing or not-knowing. Not-knowing is the same duck as the knowing duck because there's an 'I' in front of it. There is 'I' who is identified and there is an 'I' who is not identified. Both have to be false. Whatever the 'I' claims is false.

So, what is your question? Today is the last talk and I like when time runs out. It's like when people get old they go to temple and churches more and pray more. They have a feeling that if I don't do it now maybe I don't have the time anymore later. They get spiritual – just-in-case. Because soon I would be gone and I don't know what would happen and maybe there is a God, so just-in-case I pray. Just-in-case you exist, I believe in you. What do you do here? You think just-in-case the knowledge may leave you, so already now you enter the not-knowing.

Q [Another visitor]: If everything is pre-determined then basically we don't have a choice...

K: The main thing is there is maybe a choice, but no chooser. Infinite choices but no chooser. Try to find the chooser. So, there is no question of having or not having a choice. First try to find one who could have a choice or no choice. Having no choice is like saying I don't know what I am. The moment there is an 'I' having or not having a choice, understanding or not understanding, both is misunderstanding. Both depend on one who needs to know. What would come out of knowing whether there is a choice or no-choice?

Q: Everything will happen as per the destiny anyway...

K: Maybe nothing ever happened. Maybe that you believe that something ever happened is already a false experience. Then understanding that everything happens the way it has to happen is already too late. Maybe it happens or not – who cares? Who cares if there is a free-will or no free-will? Only 'me'. And only 'me' needs to know because only 'me' needs to have an advantage by understanding. Trying to get out of the me-sery of 'me' because the 'me' knows without the 'me', the 'me' is better-off. As much the 'me' tries to get rid of the 'me', the 'me' becomes real. So, you just create a dependency.

No. The only absolute way out is by being that who never went in anything. That's the problem. Your nature never went into anything. It's never born, never came out of its true nature, never came out of what-it-is. The main problem is it cannot go back because it never went out. So, it's a long way home if you have never left home. Then you are on the way and always imagine how it would be at home.

I'm pointing to the impossible going home because maybe there's no home for you; no need for home. But now you're home sick. By imagining that you're born, the belief system became real and that makes you sick. You could vomit moment-by-moment, so sick you are. Having a body is sickness. It's disease that came. Now having a body, being a body, the disease is already established. The virus is full in action. Why, why, why comes out. So, what to do with this disease?

Q: The more you try; you are in a bigger trap...

K: That's why it's called illness because it's an ill-usion that you are something that can get sick. But now by trying to get out of the illusion you establish that you are sick who needs to get out of the illusion. It's a fantastic trap made by yourself. The very best intention that you want to be healthy makes you sick. The very nice intention of knowing the truth makes you ignorant.

But they are all seekers of truth and they are very proud about it. They're sure that they are better seekers than ones seeking happiness or seeking a good life or seeking good family. They are seeking mundane things, I'm seeking truth, I'm spiritual, I'm a special seeker. I'm sicker than any other sicker. I'm the sickest of the sickest. I'm a true sicker. [Laughter] The sickness of truth came over me and the sickness of truth is the most severe sickness. You feel permanent longing for that what you even don't know what-it-is. Fantastic! What a trap!

I always adore myself for being such a good trapper; making all the fantastic traps which are impossible to miss.

Q [Another visitor]: Do you feel you are also in the trap?

K: I'm the trap. I'm the trapper, the trapping and the trapped and I cannot miss any trap. I'm the trapper, the trapping and the trapped and the trapper always steps into his own trap. And I just don't mind being trapped in the trap made by myself. It's a self-made trap. I'm the prisoner, the prison and that what is imprisoned. I'm totally addicted to what I am. I'm the addict, the addiction and what I am addicted to. I'm totally fucked – absolutely fucked by myself. The absolute fucker, fucking and being fucked. That's an absolute fact. The trinity of Shiva. Shiva being the light, the yoni and whatever comes out of it. No way out!

Q: For living the life we need sunlight of hope...

K: I have neither hope nor no-hope.

Q: After understanding this philosophy, my life has become directionless...

K: And later it would be erectionless. [Laughter] That means when something comes up, you don't go with it. You don't erect with erection. When the lingam, the light appears, you don't go with the light. You just stay where you are which is That what-you-are experiencing the light. But you don't go with the light. So, if the first lingam appears, you don't become the lingam. You don't go with the lingam and the yoni. You just stay as you are. You totally abide in That what-you-cannot-not-be which was, is and will be prior and beyond all imaginary light.

Now you are directionless, I didn't make a joke. Then you are erectionless because you don't get up when you get up. But now you get up when you get up. Now you wake up when you wake up. Now you go to sleep when you go to sleep. But I ask you to be That what does not wake up in waking up and does not go to sleep when it goes to sleep. That what is never awake or not-awake, which neither knows awakeness or sleep. Which absolutely doesn't know what-it-is or what-it-is-not. It is not someone who has no direction anymore.

Q: I feel totally confused now...

K: I hope so.

Q: Can you help me?

K: No! My absolute purpose is to bring chaos and confusion to everyone. [Laughter] Because what-you-are never needs any order, doesn't need anything to be what-it-is. And that what needs not to be confused, I have no interest about him. So, I bring total confusion and chaos to whatever I talk to. I'm a chaos-maker. Chaotic, as you are. This is freedom – chaos! No one can take it. Try to remain in chaos. This chaotic little 'me' will always need something to hold on to; some anchor, some ship, some captain, some order.

No one can remain as that what he believes to be in chaos. I'm here to talk to you so that you don't know anymore what-you-are and what-you-are-not because that's the nature of chaos. That's called crazy wisdom. Wisdom that doesn't know anymore what-is and what-is-not wisdom. That's crazy wisdom – directionlessness – not knowing what-is and what-is-not. And not one who has a direction and knows something and sits down like a chicken with eggs under his ass.

It's a very famous concept in Indian philosophy. You are like a chicken inside a shell pecking to get out and then a guru appears pecking from outside. Then when you are ready, you break free. [Laughter] At the right time a guru appears but I cannot peck my way out so a guru comes and pecks from outside – Anybody in there? [Laughter] No. You know me; I'm like a sledge hammer that destroys the eggs with the chicken. [Laughter] You are an egg of a barren hen. [Laughter]

In that sense, don't ask me because my hammer is careless. These days a new concept is quite famous that you are a caterpillar trying to be a butterfly. Then everyone dreams about being a butterfly and feels like a caterpillar now – One day as madam butterfly I'll meet my Mr. Butterfly and we'll have a butterfly relationship. [Laughter]

Q: You have so much fun with yourself...

K: With all the concepts coming out of what I Am. Ignorance is not laughing about a joke that comes out of you. This one, Karl, already is a joke. And not laughing about this joke is quite serious. Even when you are serious, it's the biggest fun ever. Someone who tries to be serious. Any moment you want to be serious, you are French. [Laughter] Germans don't like French and the French don't like the Germans. That's the joke. Imagine if everyone would like each other! [Yawning]

No one likes himself in the first place. Then trying to find one he could like. The more you find a little bit of what you like about a guy, you marry that guy. Stupidity runs everywhere. Maybe there's one person on this earth I can live with. I cannot live with myself but maybe there's someone around me I can live with. [Laughter]

Q: Then you make a mistake...

K: Yeah. Me-steak. This stake doesn't taste anymore so I need another stake. That's the mistake – Mr. Steak and Mrs. Steak having a barbecue in Hell's kitchen. Being on the grill of the devil – of separation. Marriage is a grill party.

Q [Another visitor]: Marriage is an unnatural system...

K: Why? You're married to your body now. Your inner child married your outer bones. [Laughter] I like these esoteric concepts, they're really fun. I would really miss them if they would go. My inner child, my butterfly, my whatever. [Laughter] In Australia they have an uplifting spirit festival. They should lift and never come back. [Laughter] I wish them all the best.

It's all very funny. So, don't worry that it would get boring if there is more sincerity. It's unlimited fun. Now you have a limited fun of drinking something and then having love. [Laughter] You better be drunk with what-you-are and have unlimited fun. For that you don't have to drink or stop drinking. That's the beauty of what-you-are, you don't have to stop anything. You can be stupid as you are and still be what-you-are. You can still play stupid. No problem. Maybe it's funnier than playing clever. When you play clever and you know everything, you have to be quite sincere.

Q [Another visitor]: It's easier to be stupid...

K: It's not only easier; it's your nature, more natural, better than the intellectual exercise. But if it happens, why not?

Q [Another visitor]: When you're in a middle of a calamity, how do you stay in this feeling?

K: It's not a doing. You are; and the circumstances change. But That what-you-are is uninterrupted. That doesn't need to be remembered. You don't even have to be aware about it. It's just that – you are! It is uninterrupted: there is no concept about it. That concept you don't have to defend. The concept that you don't know any concept is not a concept. It doesn't need to be defended and doesn't need to be reminded. It doesn't need to be remembered. It doesn't need anything. Establish yourself in That what never needs to be established.

Q: Do we need to do it quietly when there's nobody?

K: It doesn't need to be done. It's not a doing.

Q: Is it an understanding?

K: It's not an understanding. It's more than natural. It's just That what-you-are, which is uninterrupted and never needs any understanding. It's the Knowledge that you are which you cannot lose. By all the turbulences of your daily life, the knower can lose the center but the Knowledge that you are is uninterrupted. The knower is always fragile. That what is Omni-present, that what is your natural state which is not a state, that can be interrupted. That what-you-are cannot be disturbed by anything. The little 'me' that you believe to be is already disturbed even before disturbance happens.

This discrimination that the phantom who experiences the world is already disturbed by being a phantom. That existence that you can experience is already a doubtful existence. The existence that you have to exist in is already a doubtful existence. But that what-you-are which is prior – that which was, is and will be – there's no doubt in it because there's no doubter possible. And for the doubter, it's in his nature to doubt. What to do with him? Whatever knows daily life, whatever has a life, is doubtful. There's no way out of it. You have to experience the doubter, the doubting and that what can be doubted. But That what is the absolute experiencer is never part of that experiencing. So, you cannot get out of where you are not in.

The Absolute seer will never be seen in any scenery, and however the seer is, doesn't make the Absolute scenery more or less. That is the only thing worth being. You can call it the Absolute perception, the eye of God, the Self, the Absolute experience which is never an experience. But the experiencer that you start with in the morning is already too late.

No, that what needs to do something – no way! And That what-you-are never needs to do anything. In between there's no bridge. The phantom will never enter the Reality and Reality never came out of Reality. The Real will always be Real and the unreal will always be unreal. But the unreal permanently wants to become the Real. That's its nature: the unreal permanently inquiring into its nature but it still will be unreal. Consciousness, as unreal, investigating in its unreal nature.

[Mobile rings]

This is like consciousness. He knows how to start something but then he doesn't find the way to stop it. Your body is like a mobile phone with a battery inside. It has a battery life. It started out of the blue. But now trying to find a button where to stop it, doesn't work. It'll run out when it runs out. When the lifespan of the battery is over, the body will be gone naturally. But to get rid of it now is impossible because there's still a life tendency running it.

[Pointing at a visitor]

When I look at you, I see another thirty-five years. What was so bad in last sixty years?

Q [Another visitor]: Everyone thinks body is good...

K: I didn't say that. I say this body is a disease. I call it illness and I'm not alone, even Ramana called it as illness that came to him and one day it will be gone. But who counts the minutes? Who counts how long? If it would be thousands of years, who fucking cares? Any minute is too long and infinite time is too short.

It's always amazing, all the seekers don't want to exist but they want to become immortal. They want to live forever, but not in this body. Who fucking cares in what kind of camera position and what kind of thing you experience yourself? You'll never stop experiencing yourself. If you experience yourself as a day fly, every second counts, but now you worry about the remaining life. It's not even a glimpse of *Parabrahman*. A glimpse of *Parabrahman* is for thousands of years and now you worry about thirty-five years? And then you want to become the unborn principle which has infinite time, but you don't want another thirty-five years. What do you want? Eternity or being enlightened and being gone forever? [Laughter]

Q: I don't know what I want, where I came from and where I'm going...

K: Come on, you know what you want. You want to be enlightened. [Laughter] Look at him, now he lies so innocently. [Laughter] He's fucking greedy for enlightenment. Every cell of his body is longing for enlightenment.

Q: Yes, I spent forty years wishing about it. [Laughter] I started reading about enlightenment when I was sixteen years and it's deep-rooted in my blood. [Laughter] It's not so easy to brush it out...

K: No one wants you to brush it out. What was the first book that you read on spirituality?

Q: The title of the book was 'Om' and it mentioned that if you chant 'Om' you would be cured of diseases...

K: I would say the same... if you meditate on light and sound, the primal, it will heal all your diseases. The light and sound meditation is the most profound. Be that what-you-are which is before, during and after the sound and light, which is Om. Just be established as That which is before the first and last which is *om*: that is your very nature and that is never sick. Healing you from all your diseases, all your belief systems, all your concepts of what-you-are and what-you-are-not, is being That which is with and without the first and the last; which is Om – awareness, the light of Shiva – the first and the last notion of existence.

What-you-are is beyond or prior or with and without the purest notion of Om. Being That what-you-cannot-not-be, is health itself. No possibility of getting any sickness when you are what-you-are. That never needs to seek itself; there is no seeker in it, no longing in it. All what you claim now that is not good for you, never applies to what-you-are. Getting healed from all the belief system is just being That.

In that sense, only you can heal yourself from all misery. There's no other doctor who can heal you. Just by being what-you-are, you are totally healed from all that misery. Nothing else can heal you. The rest always makes you more sick. Every relative idea of body health and spiritual health are all part of the disease. Even understanding is a disease. Imagine! The 'understanding' disease.

Q: What I Am is already perfect?

K: What-you-are doesn't need to be perfect to be what-it-is. Perfection doesn't apply to it. It is what-it-is – imperfect and perfect. It is prior or beyond even the idea of perfection. There's no need of perfection in that what-you-are. If you say it is perfect, then you separate yourself with that what is not perfect. So, you better have no idea of what-you-are. It is not a question of perfection. It's being That what is satisfaction itself which never needs to be more satisfied as what-it-is. Whatever you do now will not make it. That what now needs to be satisfied will always be sat-is-fiction. By all that fiction, you miss yourself.

Sat has to be a fact – sat-is-faction. It's a fact that you are! Even if you deny to exist, you are. You have to be even to say, I am not. You have to know even to say, I don't know. Without the omnipresence of knowledge 'you are', there cannot be anyone who says, I know or I don't know. That knowledge cannot be learnt by anyone. You cannot attain it by learning. You cannot lose it by anything. It cannot get lost by ignorance and it cannot be gained by understanding.

If you just drop the misunderstanding, the 'me' understanding. If you could drop the 'me' understanding by being what-you-are, the absolute understanding will just remain as-it-is. But not because one understood anything. I can only kill 'you', but what-you-are, I cannot kill. If I would believe that by killing your body, by killing your whatever, it would help to be what-you-are, I would kill you right away. If I would believe that the absolute Self needs you to go to be what-it-is, I would shoot you on first sight. But the Absolute what-you-are is in spite of presence or absence what-it-is. That kills the idea that one has to go for you to be what-you-are.

That's the absolute killing, that nothing has to go or to be killed to be that what is Absolute. If something had to go, it would still be relative because it needs something to go to be Absolute. The Absolute absolutely doesn't mind if you exist or not. It's absolutely irrelevant for what-you-are. If you exist for thirty-five years more, or thirty-five thousand years or thirty-five billion years more, it would not lose anything by that and it would never mind. I can only point to that what never minds.

This carelessness which can never be learnt by anyone. It's not like someone now sits down and says; 'Now I don't care anymore'. [Laughter] I don't know and I don't care that I don't know and I don't care that I don't care. [Laughter] Whatever happens, I don't care. I just try to present what normally people try to do. From now on, I hate everything.

Q [Another visitor]: So, meditation doesn't help?

K: I didn't say that. It's not about help. Meditation needs to be done in the right way. What is the right way of meditating?

Ninety-nine percent of meditators are meditating out of expectation. Meditating on peace, meditating on understanding, meditating on whatever comes into you, meditating on a good marriage. Both only meditating, they don't see each other anymore, that's the best marriage ever. [Laughter]

What would you say is the right way of meditating?

Q: Focus and reach that what you expect...

K: No. That is expectation.

Q: But the expectation is to come out of the expectation...

K: But that is still expectation. You meditate on getting rid of the intention. The intention to get rid of the intention is not meditation. Meditation is action without expectation, without intention at all.

Q [Another visitor]: Can we call it witnessing?

K: No. I don't call it anything at all. You can just call it action without intention, sitting without a sitter.

Q: Why can we not call it witnessing?

K: Witnessing is still too much because then there is one who thinks that witnessing is better than observing. There's an intention in it, there's an advantage – witnessing is better than observing or being something which is observed. Just be that what-you-are in action and there's nothing to come out of it. That's meditation.

Q [Another visitor]: In the early stages, Ramana also meditated with intention...

K: No. He said meditation is action without intention. That is consciousness meditating without the intention to know consciousness. That's the meditation of consciousness – absolute action without any intention of anything. But that cannot be done and it's not attractive for the little 'me'. Because the 'me' always needs a goal, it needs something to achieve. That's not meditation. So, it cannot be exercised. It's not training. It's 24 by 7 everyday. Every moment you meditate because that is your nature. Right now consciousness is the meditation of the Absolute. The Absolute realizing itself, the Absolute meditating about itself. But without any expectation of a result. It cannot get more Absolute as it is.

In spite of whatever way the dream is dreamt, it cannot get

more or less. That is meditation, as consciousness. Everything else is heavy work for the 'me'. A 'me' trying to work out something and calling it meditation. Especially sitting somewhere for two hours is not meditation. Any moment there is a meditator involved, it's not meditation. It's sitting with an expectation that by sitting you get more peaceful or become more understanding. I can meditate myself away – it's like trying to get rid of the 'me' meditation. Because you want to get rid of something what you don't like – 'me'. That is meditation with intention. That's personal meditation because there's an expectation of a result. Maybe I meditate so much that I enter the witness state. Then I'll be better-off. It all sounds good. And actually being a witness is an advantage for the 'me'. The witness is better than being an observer or the observed. The witness state is already awareness. It's all fine. But who needs to be fine? Say it...

Q: Me...

K: It's always me. If you could stay there in awareness, it would be fine. But there will always be an intense circumstance that will get you out of there – if you like it or not. The shares drop and the stock market collapses and suddenly the witness state is gone. [Laughter] The witness state is fragile, it's all fragile. Nothing is stable enough, not sound enough. It sounds good. But whatever sounds good, is never sound enough. Taoism says whatever sounds beautiful is not the truth. Whatever sounds good is not good enough. It's never sound enough. Any state is a fragile one.

Q: What you mentioned is at the highest level. As a beginner, you need to have an intention...

K: It's too late when you are a beginner. When there's a beginner, there's no end. When there's a beginning, there's a never ending story of a beginner who wants to become what-he-is. That's the story of consciousness because consciousness begins and infinitely tries to know itself. These ideas of Vedanta, that you have to do something and step-by-step you make it, sounds good. It gives hope. But who needs that hope? Do you really think the Absolute needs hope?

I know you want to find recipes but not here. Cooking with Karl means cooking without recipes. [Laughter]

Q: Somewhere there has to be an initiation...

K: The initiation comes by itself, the action comes by itself, everything comes by itself; not by you.

Q: Suppose I give you an apple and a knife, how would you eat without cutting?

K: I would throw it on your head. [Laughter] That would be eating without a knife.

Q: You need to initiate an action...

K: No. I'm never hungry. How can you make that what-you-are hungry? Only the 'me' is hungry, and the 'me' is infinitely hungry. It will never be satisfied and all your concepts now to try to satisfy the 'me' never work.

I can only repeat what all the guys before said – The Self is already attained and that who wants to attain the Self now, will never attain the Self. No way! Whatever has a beginning will never attain that what never had any beginning. How can that what has a beginning attain that what never had any beginning? How can that what is born enter that what is unborn principle? That what is born is already dead. How can that what is dead become alive? By what steps? It's like a dead corpse needs a beginning and then it will be alive again? The dead will always remain the dead. That is deathly sure and that what is life is always life. Otherwise you only see zombies, walking tombstones who want to become life in the cemetery of this universe.

Again and again and again and again, there's nothing to gain from anything for what-you-are. And again and again and again, all empty moments, all empty sensations. No gaining, no losing, again and again. But you make it a gain, I want a gain, I want to have more. I'm not satisfied with my little one. I want to be a big one. I'm now a personal consciousness and I want to be a cosmic consciousness – 'me'. I want to expand into the infinite – 'me'. The business has to expand. My personal shop is not good enough; I want to satisfy myself universally.

Everyone reads the books from being a little one to the big one. And everyone says – me too! When will I be cosmic? For me it's being a little comic to a big comic.

Q: How can we function without a 'me'?

K: Every night you function without a 'me'. The heart is beating, the brain is pumping blood but there's no one who hears. Now you claim to be the one who makes a story out of these experiences. Every night there are experiences without anyone making a story out of it. The 'me', the caretaker of the story is sometimes there and sometimes not. But the story is still there without your story maker. No one needs your little diary.

Q: That's in the night. What about the day? [Laughter]

K: Everyone is a nightmare for himself even during the daytime. If it would not be a nightmare, you would not try to get out of it. If this would be a pleasant dream, everything would be fine. No one would try to get out of this pleasant dream. You only become a seeker when you become a nightmare; the 'me' is unbearable. Then you suddenly say I don't like this dream anymore.

If everything runs fine, your wife is not having sex with your neighbor, or at least you don't know about it. [Laughter] And your divorce doesn't cost you all your money and your life is fine and your car is running and your employer is not firing you, then maybe you can handle it. But then if something happens, you say 'I don't want it anymore. Now I don't like it anymore. I want to find a way out. Life is not doing what I want.'

Existence is a toilet, it takes everything. It never minds what comes. If you want to have a pointer to what is your nature, be as a toilet because the toilet doesn't mind what ass sits on it. [Laughter] All seven states can sit on you and it gives a shit. That's Ranjit –

Be the zero-zero, accepting whatever. Toilet accepts whatever shit comes.

Q [Another visitor]: What about intuition? Is it in the same category as witnessing?

K: It's the same shit. [Mocking] Anyway only women have intuition, we as men should not talk about it. Women have emotions and intuitions, all what we don't need. [Laughter] We have it but we don't talk about it. No, whatever you call it is the same toilet.

Q: Intuition has no time in it, it is instantaneous...

K: Who makes a difference?

Q: Hopefully there's no 'me' in that...

K: But it needs one who makes a difference between time and no-time. Who calls no-time as intuition and time as intention? Who defines that? It needs a definer who defines as with and without 'me'. When there's no 'me', he says its intuition and when there's a 'me' that's intention. It needs a definer, one who makes differences. You can call it Consciousness... Consciousness wants to be finer. It's never fine enough. Is there any final in it? So, you already get fined by trying to define it.

It's like trying to find the end of Shiva's light. You want to go to the deepest truth and the highest level of Self. Then you define the Self as levels. You get fined by being relative. You're already punished by trying to find the end of existence. You define existence. You already get a ticket for parking on a wrong place because wherever you park, you still have a car. Even a bicycle is too much. You're a king who wants to park and always wants to have the free parking space – by the power of intuition.

All these trainings, they power you something relative. You will control that and you will always have enough and blah, blah, blah. The devil works very hard by promising you something to keep you in the relative need. If it doesn't work anymore, then the devil asks you to meditate. You make yourself all empty promises.

Then I will be better-off, then I will be different, then, then, then, then – always then. Always postponing because without postponing something, you cannot remain the little 'me' you are. That's the power of later – then. If I sit long on the bench then I will one day fall like Eckhart and be in the 'now'. [Laughter] There will be a new earth, then I will transform myself into my true nature – then. But first we have to work on the new earth, we have to transform our human consciousness to the higher level of oneness, then everyone would wake up. Then and then and then...

All the teachers need 'then', because without future goal, without future promise, no one would do anything. But I'm a Zen master – Zen and Zen and Zen, there's never-ending Zen. And it will never be enough. There was a book on Zen called 'Zen – The Biggest Lie Ever' from the biggest Zen master from Japan.

The toilet needs some shit...

Q [Another visitor]: Then some flushing...

K: Enlightenment flush; then all my shit will be gone. Then for a while the toilet is without an ass on it. But then comes another ass, then the toilet is occupied again. It's a nice expectation that if I get rid of this ass, I will be a free toilet. But the moment you are free, there is a queue as long as eternity that is waiting to sit on you again. [Laughter] You kick out one ass and another ass comes. And you never know if the next ass is a bigger ass.

You are the Absolute ass and you have infinite ass-holes. But now you believe that you are one ass-hole. But you are the Absolute ass that has many holes. The absolute has infinite camera positions from where everything comes out.

Q [Another visitor]: What is being said here seems like a technique of *neti-neti*, neither-neither...

K: If you establish yourself in *neti-neti*, neither this nor that. If you can stay in that for whatever time, sooner or later the 'me' is annihilated. It ceases away, it cannot stay. It can only stay when it is that or that – knowing or the not-knowing. But if it's neither the knowing nor the not-knowing – *neti-neti* – the 'me', the 'knower' cannot remain. The claimer cannot claim anything in *neti-neti* because nothing is his. It becomes like an absolute eraser.

Q: It's like you flush it out...

K: It's a *neti-neti* flush, whatever shit comes – flush! It's like things come in from one side and they go out from the other. It's like an absolute openness, inside-outside. There's nothing in between that filters it. It's in-out, in-out, in-out.

But the moment you have a concept of a healthy food or a good understanding, then you again collect that shit. Then you become a shit collector, that's called 'me': the 'me' needs to collect shit. What would the first shit – 'me' – do without the collection of shit? What would that experience of 'I' do without a collection of experiences which is his collection? In *neti-neti* nothing works and in that the chain of sensations breaks. They cannot remain, they have no substance anymore. If nothing is neither good nor bad – *neti-neti*. Without that polarity, that what lives from two cannot survive; if you could do that! Maybe it works; there is no guarantee in anything. Maybe it takes one year, two years, a hundred years, a thousand years, you will never know. It will work, but maybe not in the time frame that you expect. Because the mind will always be clever enough to make another concept out of *neti-neti*. That's the danger in it.

Neti-neti is not a concept of the mind. It is just remaining in that what-you-are. It's a silent *neti-neti*. It's not like someone says – 'not this, no this': there's no one who says 'no'. It just remains in that what-it-is. Abiding in the Self – that's self-abidance. Abiding in That what never needs to abide in anything, what never needs any concept of any kind to be. That what is not a concept, that is *neti-neti*. You're neither that nor That. That means that you are the undecided. Being the undecided, you have no sides. There is no this side or that side – being the undecided. You have no inside and no outside – neither in nor outside, that what-you-are.

Undecided Neti-Neti

Being the absolute not knowing, the absolute unknown, absolute undecided. Establishing yourself in that by being that. Abiding in That what never needs to abide in anything, that's *neti-neti*. It's not like the concept 'me' trying to clean something, like a broom that wants to wipe out all concepts. In that, the first concept that wipes out all the concepts remain and hence it may not work.

Neti-neti has no owner of anything. Neither owns nor doesn't own – always undecided. It's never 'yes' or 'no'. It's neither 'yes' nor 'no'. He's neither inside nor outside. Whatever comes up – neither. If you could stay in the neither, abiding in that is your natural state. This is your natural state: everything else would just dissolve by itself. Don't use it as a personal concept, but you're tempted to use it as one. It's not like a work or technique. It's like meditation. The meditation of *neti-neti* means being the undecided. It's not like having an intention that now I would like to have a peaceful mind or I want to reach enlightenment. The *neti-neti* is neither enlightenment nor not enlightenment. You absolutely don't know if you are or if you're not.

Undecided – neither enlightened nor unenlightened. Who fucking cares? That carelessness of *neti-neti* I talk about. The rest is just finding something and telling the friend that I found home. It's like one gets enlightened, then he tells his friend that you can do it too. Whatever you can present is not worth presenting and the Presence you-are will never present itself. The Presence you-are is that *neti-neti*. It never shows up. That's your Buddha nature – *neti-neti* – undecided. Neither this or that or anything. That's Tao. In Tao, there's no Yin and no Yang. That what is unborn is ever young, never becomes Yin. [Laughter]

Q [Another visitor]: It is neither nothing, nor everything...

K: Neither-neither. Whatever one claims to be, for sure is not *neti-neti*.

Q: There are statements made that it is nothing and everything. That is a wrong statement...

K: I know. That's how books are written, like the power of now. If you say this is power of now you objectify something. That you can understand. But if it's neither 'now' nor not the 'now', what then? What to do? *Neti-neti.*

Everyone wants to understand it and employ it for its own advantage. You cannot employ *neti-neti* for your personal advantage. It doesn't work because *neti-neti* is not made for work, it's made for laziness. [Laughter]

Q [Another visitor]: Can it be maybe-maybe?

K: No.

Q: 'Maybe' as in undecided...

K: In maybe, you already decided to be a maybe. No. That is like positive thinking. People think maybe I'm everything, maybe I'm nothing. It leaves you with a possibility that 'I' can be everything and 'I' can be nothing. Maybe I'm everything, maybe I'm nothing. But if you're neither-neither, the 'me' cannot survive. In 'maybe', it can maybe survive. [Laughter] The baby cannot be killed by maybe. It's not for nothing they made it *neti-neti* and not maybe-maybe. Maybe is a state of mind. *Neti-neti* is neither mind nor no-mind. There is mind, no-mind, never mind. That's *neti-neti.*

Q [Another visitor]: Whenever I listen to your talks, I forget about everything. Isn't this meditation?

K: Yeah, forgetfulness. But it's still fullness. Only a fool remembers that he didn't remember.

Q: But that happens naturally...

K: What doesn't happen naturally? Show me one thing that doesn't happen naturally. Naturally, one is stupid. By nature you are knowledge but naturally you're stupid. And knowledge doesn't mind to be stupid or not stupid. It neither minds nor doesn't mind to be stupid. Right now we all sit here being stupid. But what to do?

That what is neither sitting here nor not sitting here, never minds. But that one who is sitting here, for sure is stupid. Then the one, who claims I'm not sitting here, is still stupid. I'm here but I'm not here. It's like being somebody but not nobody. It all sounds very nice but it's just a phrase; trying to be positive. Be positive, don't try to be positive. Be positive is your nature.

Q [Another visitor]: What do you mean by be the positive?

K: *Neti-neti* means negative-negative. In that the positive remains unpronounced. It doesn't need anything. But everything is negative-negative. If someone asks you, are you the Self? Negative. Are you not the Self? Negative. Are you God? Negative. Are you not God? Negative. That's called undecided. It's so easy when you are it; and you are it anyway.

Knowing is a disease, it makes you dizzy.

Q [Another visitor]: Do you ever meditate?

K: 24 by 7. I cannot not meditate. I'm 24 by 7 that what is meditation. I cannot leave meditation. 24 by 7 I'm that what is consciousness. Consciousness is meditation. The nature of consciousness is meditation, the absolute meditating about itself. Meditation is the nature of what I am. You can also say I am the nature of meditation, whichever way you look at it. Uninterrupted. Never comes, never goes.

In that what is Reality, there is no-moment without realization. The realization of Reality is Reality meditating about itself. Every experience or non-experience is meditation about what-you-are – uninterrupted. The presence or the absence, whatever you experience, is the eternal meditation about that what-you-are. In that way, meditation is self-realization. The Self experiencing itself in infinite possibilities of presences and absence. There's no special meditation. It is 24 by 7 by 365.

Q: Prior to this stage?

K: There is no prior to this stage. That's your natural state. Prior to your nature, there is no prior and no beyond. There's no before and there's no after. Whatever has a before and an after, meditates and counts the years and hours, is never good enough, the personal meditation, even if there's an intention of meditating on truth. In Avadhut Gita Dattatreya calls them shamelessly meditating! Shame on you that you still meditate with intention. I call it crime against yourself, whoever sits down with an intention and meditates about a personal advantage, by whatever way. Even meditating for truth, which is an advantage for him, is a crime against yourself. It's a criminal act against yourself, against your nature. It's a crime and you would be punished for that. And you are punished for that!

Any moment you have an expectation from what you think is yours again, with the imaginary doership or non-doership, you are punished by not being what-you-are. That is the most severe punishment which can only be given by yourself.

Q: But sometimes I feel relaxation in meditation...

K: It's a crime of relaxation because you take that relaxation as an advantage for what-you-are. That's a crime.

Q: Are you saying not to relax?

K: I didn't say that. I said taking that as a personal advantage gives you all the disadvantages that come with it. I have nothing against it but nothing for it either. You decide yourself. If you have sides and if you decide what is better for you, relaxation is better than no relaxation, then you have sides. The moment you have sides, you are a relative object of time and that is depressed, you are under pressure of time. Then you have the precious time in front of you and you're always pressing and pressing. Then sometimes you're in deep depression of no-time. All what comes by that story.

Q [Another visitor]: Why is it so difficult to know our absolute nature?

K: It's not only difficult, it's impossible. If you could know your nature, there would be two natures. Only the nature which is without the second nature is worth to be. But if you need to know yourself to be yourself, you make yourself depending on the relative knowledge. That's already a crime against yourself because you make yourself a relative object that can be known in time. You separate yourself by trying to know yourself.

I tell you be happy that you cannot know yourself. Enjoy that you can never know yourself. That is the *neti-neti*, the undecided Absolute which can never know itself. It can neither know nor not know itself. It is Absolute knowledge but it will never know itself in any relative way because it has no sides.

Q: But then why do we forget to be happy?

K: Because you want to be happy. By wanting to be happy, you make yourself unhappy. You have an intention for yourself. You have an intention of knowledge, an intention of happiness. By that intention, instant unhappiness. That's the way you realize yourself, you cannot help it. This trap is always there. The moment you wake up there is a lover and its intention is to know the beloved. How to stop that?

In that sense one tells you, don't wake up when waking up happens because what-you-are is not what wakes up. When sleep happens, you are not that what falls asleep. You're neither awake nor not awake. You're neither sleep nor not asleep. Stay in that neither-neither, *neti-neti*. That *neti-neti* never wakes up in waking up and never has any intention of knowing anything because it is knowledge and never left knowledge. But even calling it knowledge is too much. It's neither knowledge nor not knowledge – neither-neither. Because it doesn't know any knowledge. It doesn't know any joy. If you call it joy, it's already too much.

I would not call it anything. But it's meant to be that they call it *Paramatma* or *Parabrahman*, call it whatever: I like to call it underwear, stinky socks! [Laughter] That's the beauty of what-you-are, it never minds what you call it. It never reacts to it. It neither reacts nor doesn't react. You can call it the biggest asshole of all times and there's silence, there's no reaction. Call it whatever! For me calling it stinking socks is quite okay. So, if you ask me what's my name, my name is stinking socks.

Q [Another visitor]: Bhagavat Gita says whenever there is absence of religion and mankind is in disorder, God will appear and save mankind. What is the pointer?

K: I think the translation is not right. The translation should be when there is a human vessel with no religion anymore, no concept of his being, there's no God, there's no devil, there's no higher, there's no lower. The absolute absence of any religion means there's no way to God or home or anything. In the emptiness of that vessel, God already is.

When you have no religion anymore, absolute absence of any religion, of any belief system of what-you-are and what-you-are-not, being absolute undecided, God is already there in its absolute nature, because that's the nature of God, the nature of Brahman, the nature of Self. But any moment there's one religion left, of truth, of Self, of God, the toilet is occupied. God doesn't go on an occupied toilet, he wants to have a toilet without a religion, the zero-zero. That's the nature of the Absolute.

God doesn't arrive, when it's zero-zero, God is already there! It's not like when there is no humanity or no religion, God arrives. No. If there's one vessel where there's zero-zero then God is already there, not knowing God, just being That! Ranjit also pointed to the Absolute zero-zero. It's not entering, it's not an emptiness you can imagine, it's not an absence of religion you can imagine.

Q [Another visitor]: The 24 by 7 by 365 of self-realization also includes the phantom?

K: Absolutely. 24 by 7 by 365 going through all the possibilities, infinitely. And none of them is better than the other one because you are undecided. When you're undecided, the first is as good as the seventh or the fifth. You are undecided because you don't know what is good or bad in any of the states. This carelessness, that's your nature because none of that makes you more or less as you are. None of them gives you anything or takes anything away. They're all dream states. All seven ways of realizing yourself but you cannot get more or less real by any one of them. That is what you are, the Absolute who can never get less Absolute or more Absolute by anything.

So, bye-bye. Don't buy anything, not even from yourself. You're not a seller and you're not a buyer.

12th November 2014, 2nd Talk
Mumbai, India

www.ingramcontent.com/pod-product-compliance
Lightning Source LLC
Chambersburg PA
CBHW070736160426
43192CB00009B/1460